HEART IN GEAR

HEART IN GEAR

CHRISTOPHER HOFFMANN

Copyright © 2017 by Christopher Hoffmann

All rights reserved. This book or any portion thereof
may not be reproduced or used in any manner whatsoever
without the express written permission of the publisher
except for the use of brief quotations in a book review.

Printed in the United States of America

First Printing, 2017

ISBN 978-0-9990875-0-3

Christopher Hoffmann
2916 SE Belmont
Portland, OR 97214

www.HeartInGear.com

CONTENTS

Introduction	vii

PART ONE: KNOCKOUT

Face Plant	3
Niagaras	8
A Father's Quiet Rage	15
Encounter with a Tantrika	19
The Box I Built	28
First Date in Eighteen Years	30
THUD	38

PART TWO: BUILDER

Inventor Child	45
On Being Invincible	47
The Marketplace in Nature	55
Building my Alter Ego	59
The Mattress	62

PART THREE: LETTING GO

It Needs to Scale	69
Learning to Lead	73
Finding My Inner Rhythm	77
Honesty is All We Have	81
Call in the Project Manager	84
A Test of Faith in Shenzhen	88

PART FOUR: MY EROTIC AWAKENING

The Erotic Ball	97
Normal Boyfriend Behavior	104
Boundaries	110
Mac-and-Cheese	115
Just Three Hours Once a Week	119
Second Tantrika Visit	126

PART FIVE: FREE NAVIGATION

Punked in Stockholm	135
Getting it Right	145
Life Contains an Ending	152
Handing Each Other Back	158
Two Candles	160
Calling Forth Our Futures	164
Acknowledgement	169

INTRODUCTION

I had no idea what I was doing, but I was more relentless than the voices in my head that told me to stop. After pounding out 50,000 words, I signed up for a Meetup group for aspiring writers. It was a dozen women, plus a few men that agreed to read each other's work, edit it, and share feedback every two weeks. Immediately, I had my ass handed to me. The feedback ranged from straight-up hating my work, to tepidly trying to figure out what the hell I was trying to accomplish. After showing up to this group for three months, one of the men, whom I found interesting in an esoteric sort of way, finally got it.

"Look," he announced to the group, "this is a book targeted at men. Men need to feel the visceral, frank, over-the-shoulder vantage point of what it's like to be a man trying to figure himself out."

He looked at me and continued.

"Focus on why all of your erotic details matter," he said. "Stop trying to make things so complicated. You're a great storyteller—just focus on why we should care, and what each lesson is." I literally wept out loud in front of everyone from the sheer release of finally being understood. Maybe all this emotional purging onto paper could actually have value for someone. Maybe I was driven to write this all down for a reason.

Stories are interesting things. They can act as a fabric that knits our reality together, a fabric we can rely on to protect us. They can also liberate us like cell door skeleton keys that free us to walk into an unknown future. I couldn't help but wonder: of all the hundreds of wild stories I've lived to tell, why had only a select few stayed with me? Over the years I'd find myself retelling them with a bit more detail as I slowly became conscious of their true meaning. Imbedded in them was some form of life lesson I needed to know—some need to act out physically what I was feeling in my psyche.

Our culture demands that men climb some form of ladder to success, and to surround ourselves with visual cues of our affluence. Then we're left alone to defend our position in the hierarchy. I fell victim to this too. I had no idea how dependent I was on my pop-up store self-image. I couldn't separate the desire for comfort from the need to define my social standing. If anyone tried to marginalize my position or suggest that my polish wasn't as shiny as the next guy's, I was quick to defend myself. I was hopelessly held hostage by the self-promoting stories I told myself, and how they defined what I thought I was allowed to do.

During my 20-year marriage, even though I accomplished a lot, I had not done a single "story-worthy" thing. I'm not talking "what did you do last weekend?" stories; I'm talking life-changing, holy-fuck-I-can't-believe-I-made-it-out-alive stories. And looking back on those 20 years, I noticed that the quality of experience that now drew me, and the types of encounters that intrigued my intellect, had evolved.

What felt edgy, or even fear-inducing, was no longer thrashing on a punk rock stage looking into a mosh pit, but something bigger—like, what would it take to extend my creative drive, build a team, and start a company? What I found visually captivating had evolved as well. I wasn't into the "ivory tower" canon of classic art, but more interested in what common street artists, performance artists, and drag queens could create to shine a counterculture light on the escalating homogenization of our society.

How I saw my life was shifting too, and how I wanted to 'retell myself' was evolving. I've always been some form of risk taker, but this evolution or transition away from being a traditional engineer to a more insightful and open-minded innovator is what allowed me to raise $2.3 million in angel investor funding to start RYNO Motors, the single wheel electric motorcycle company. My embodiment allowed me to relax into my being. As a result, others trusted me.

Over the year it took to write and drive this book to completion, I went through a few tough periods as RYNO's footing faltered. Already feeling the pressure to keep RYNO Motors on a steady glide path, I struggled with the voices that tried to convince me I was a total poser as a writer. I feared that if I released such a vulnerable and erotically-charged book and it sucked, it would ruin my entire career as an engineer, making it impossible to fall back on that lifelong trajectory to sustain myself.

In a small rented room with a bed, I faced the depth of that fear—and kept writing.

It was through the process of putting my history down on paper that I discovered the stories I'd been telling myself about my life, and who I was, were all bullshit. This took me by surprise. I would put something down about my dad's rage, or the way my ex-wife wanted me to stand inside a symbolic box, or how I needed to dim my light so people would like me; then I'd see how it was my own fear, or poor choices, that held me back. As I wrote and reflected, I slowly started re-conceptualizing and rewriting my entire storyline legacy about where I thought I came from, and what I thought my role in it was.

I slowly started freeing myself from being a victim of my own limitations: from the shame of my full erotic expression; from the need to constantly wonder what others thought of me; and from worrying about whether or not I was hurting them. It was exhausting at times, but I was getting stronger by the day, and becoming clearer in who I am.

I believe the writing of this book has taught me to be a better man and a better leader, someone who values a calm and quiet approach in a state of curiosity. It is through this curiosity, and a dedication to being transparent, that eventually allowed me to enact the bold and powerful decisions needed to navigate the complexities that my company and my life demanded.

I have lived my professional life as an innovative engineer and provider, and my private life as a provocateur, creator, and explorer. No stranger to bold action, as an author I instinctively threw myself into writing to make sense of my life and my emerging new identity. As I leaned into my new improvisational landscape, I felt a need to come to grips with my erotic expression as a Rosetta Stone to understand what was emerging. Without the understanding of how our erotic nature helps us make contact with our embodied self-awareness, I knew I would never be able to feel my way forward. As I groped into the shadows of childhood shame and trauma, I tried to put my experiences into some logical metaphors or rationale to make sense of them.

I now see my erotic nature as the vibrating reed in a musical instrument. The quality of the vibration is what causes my music to sing; the shape of the resonator is what gives it tone and color. Without the vibration to strike against the form, we are simply an empty, quiet instrument sitting in a dusty case on the dark shelf of a pawn shop.

This erotic, creative drive toward exploration was like a moth attracted to ever brighter lights. At an early age, I developed a high tolerance for the ambiguous unknown. In my 20s, I found myself playing in punk bands, building a recording studio, checking out peep shows, sex clubs, and costume parties, riding motorcycles, rebuilding numerous hot rods, not to mention a piece of crap Jaguar. Then on to to New York City for four years to try to get over my ego as a singer-songwriter, and to eventually build sets for Broadway shows. During that time, I could definitely feel myself, but what I lacked was a way to calm down and integrate my wild side into a focused, open-hearted, consciously wakened man.

During the writing of this book, after hundreds of thousands of unused words, day after day of emotional confrontation with myself, I found I'd inadvertently documented my erotic self-awakening. Once I arrived at the clarity of my true potential, I realized that until I had returned from a journey of my own creation—complete with the full expression of who I am, along with financially resourced independence—I would not know myself in a state of love and autonomy. It is from this awareness, with the clarity of what my true gifts are to the world, that I continue to claim my choices, and offer my commitments to those I love—because they deserve nothing less, and I deserve nothing less.

Through this work, I have discovered a form of vulnerable experiential modeling that proposes our erotic expression is tied directly to our instinctual creative innovation. We cannot present our greatest gifts to the world until we first feel what we want to create in our bodies.

These insights expose how the fear-based culture we're stuck with will never give us the strength we need to flourish. It is NOT our ego, but our limitless CURIOSITY to make new discoveries, in harmony with our courage to be TRANSPARENT with others, which gives us strength.

Through this transparency, I now share my experiences.

What follows is an arc of what it's like to go from an up-in-my-head engineer, through the process of leaving a life that no longer served me, entering the uncharted abyss of the unknown, dozens of erotic encounters, then finally getting it right—only to realize I was hiding in that love. I woke to the reality that until I had the courage to let my true love go, out of respect and trust of what this love deserved, I was never going to gain the strength to face the real pain of claiming my full and autonomous sovereignty of self.

In certain sections of the book, stories appear chronologically; in others, thematically. In certain stories I have changed the names of people out of respect for them and their unique journeys. Rather than getting caught up in the "what happens next?" or "do I know this person?"

nature of things, I want readers to *feel* their way through the narrative as much as possible.

On the island of Grinda in the archipelago off Stockholm, Sweden, hangs a little sign in a coffee shop: "Bad decisions often make good stories." The stories I share here aren't so much bad decisions as they are human decisions. This distinction is the inquisitive sentiment I sit with as I release this book out into the world.

With gratitude and my heart now in gear,

Chris Hoffmann

Whether married or single, and regardless of gender expression, my hope is for all of us to claim our own unique form of freedom—for ourselves and for the world—as our most heroic act of rebellion.

PART 1:
KNOCKOUT

We called it the RYNO bike. It balanced front to back using a gyro stabilized electric motor, but the first prototype was too heavy and hard to twist—basically un-rideable. Six months later, on the first day of testing a new steering system on Prototype Two, my software guy and I made a pact: if we couldn't ride it, we were done. To our amazement, our single-wheeled wonder rode like a magic carpet. We were blown away by the breakthrough. We spun toward each other, and nearly in unison said, "Holy Shit! Now we're in trouble."

Face Plant

If it wasn't for that flimsy bike helmet, I would have died right there. The violence of my jaw hitting the pavement was so forceful it fractured in two places, split my chin open, shattered four teeth and broke parts off four others. My hands pounded into the pavement so hard, bones were sticking out the backs of my fists.

I climbed up on all fours to find myself spitting out teeth and blood. My jaw was sideways in my mouth. As people started crowding around, I crawled over to the grass and rolled on my back, then fumbled as best I could to free my cell phone from my pocket and call my wife, Jean. All I could say was, "I'm hurt," and gave her the cross streets.

Later, in all the confusion of paramedics shining flashlights in my eyes, lifting me on a back board, and asking me what day of the week it was, I never saw Jean drive up. As they were loading me into the ambulance I caught sight of her out of the corner of my eye. She was standing frozen in the middle of the street, surrounded by firetrucks, flashing lights, the bark of the dispatch radio, and a growing crowd of spectators.

I had been riding the RYNO fairly regularly, each day after dinner. I'd become a sort of folk hero around the neighborhood. People I never met before would yell, "Hey, RYNO Man!" as I rode by.

The original idea for the RYNO actually came from our daughter, Lauren, when she was 13-years-old. Driving out on one of our monthly fishing trips, she mentioned she'd seen a one-wheel motorcycle in a video game.

"Could something like that actually be built?" she wondered aloud.

"What does it look like?" I asked.

Lauren drew a sketch and showed it to me as we drove. We talked about it for a while, and when we got home I did some web searches. As a seasoned inventor, I had done the classic "I'm going to be a millionaire" dance in the kitchen so many times, I knew enough to kill this idea as soon as possible. Problem was, I kept finding parts and components for it. Unable to kill it, I soon found myself intoxicated by the same ego-driven invincibility of my youth. Even at work, I was drawing sketches, trying to fit all the electronic parts into a cohesive design. My engineer's brain had not been this in touch with the thrill of victory in a long time. Just projecting into that future felt GOOD.

To wrap my head around the physics of riding on one wheel, I chopped my mountain bike in half and put a seat over the back wheel to see if I could ride it. This seemingly ridiculous endeavor proved that if I could eliminate the need to pedal by adding a gyro-stabilized motor, I could have a breakthrough product on my hands.

I kept looking for any roadblock that would stop me. With 15 years of designing factory size machines for the auto industry, I could design my way out of nearly any complicated mechanical challenge. Being a responsible family man, all that was left was a good solid logical reason why I should do this, one that would carry me forward.

A few weeks later, I showed up at a night class at the local high school machine shop, and began to tiptoe my way toward Frankensteining the first prototype together. When the shop teacher made the rounds and asked what I wanted to fabricate, I unfolded my wrinkled sketch out onto my work bench. His eyes widened and lingered for a few seconds. Then he chuckled a little.

"Good luck with that."

It took me a year to build the first one-wheel prototype. The RYNO looked like a Ducati motorcycle sawed in half: the seat placed over the big fat rear tire, the handlebars replacing the gas tank.

On the night of the accident, Lauren had headed over to a friend's house after dinner. I'd been finishing the dishes, and asked Jean if she wanted to go to bed early and light some candles. We were in couples therapy. One of our "assignments" was to make intimacy a high priority. Jean's answer came pretty quickly.

"Tonight is *Desperate Housewives*," she said—without even a hint of irony. It was her ritual: get stoned, settle into her program, and zone out.

I figured that was that, and took off on my one-wheeled motorcycle. What I didn't know was the cable that connected the micro-processor to the gyro stabilization chip had wiggled out of position. The gyro's job was to locate the center of the earth, and communicate a balance-angle to the motor controller board to keep the bike upright. Without the gyro, the processor had no idea what direction was up. "Thinking" it was falling, it pitched forward with a hammer blow to the ground at 14 miles per hour. My face took the full force of the impact, with my body and the bike right behind.

After a violent accident, there's a moment when the world comes to a sudden halt. We realize we are conscious, and slowly take stock of our limbs and ability to move. There's a shallow stillness. What's broken, bent, twisted? Then comes the lunge back toward life—nothing like spitting out teeth and blood to wake yourself up from a long, unconscious haze.

My face hitting the pavement was the last in a series of punches—my dad had died in the previous year; my best friend, Dave Lee, had killed himself three weeks earlier; I'd been unemployed for months; and my marriage was in a death spiral. The RYNO was the one thing I'd come to trust and believe in—THE THING I thought would make me famous! But even *it* had other plans.

The fall turned out to be a portal into a whole new chapter of my life, but I was in too much shock and pain at the time to see it.

After returning from the hospital, my wounds sewn up, and my hands bulk-wrapped in bandages, I fell into bed and slept. I had three days to wait before they wired my jaw shut.

The next morning, I forced myself out of bed. Jean mentioned someone from the neighborhood had dragged the RYNO back and put it inside our side gate. I shuffled over to the window and looked at the bike on its side in the pouring rain. Something about the sight of it called to me, like an alien spacecraft had crashed into my driveway. I stood there for a long time looking at the bike. With both hands broken, I couldn't even drag its metallic carcass out of the rain into the back studio to keep the electronics from getting wet.

Jean stood behind me.

"I hope you're done now," she said. Her voice was condescending. I turned as she headed toward the living room with a basket of clothes. Our eyes met in a challenging stare as she disappeared down the hall. She hated the RYNO—not for the distraction it posed in our marriage, but because it fed my bloated ego. She poked at me whenever I boasted to friends about my big ideas, taking it upon herself to remind me I should just let people discover me on their own. She was an introvert, and was probably embarrassed by my compulsive attempts to feel important. She never took the time to ask me why I had such a hunger to be seen.

I called my software engineer to tell him what had happened. He was quiet, noticeably humbled, and deeply sorry. After that I called a friend to come over and help me drag the bike into my back studio. Later that afternoon, out of nowhere, a big colorful fruit basket arrived—a gift from my software engineer. Known for his dry humor, his note read:

"I hope you have a blender for all the smoothies you'll be drinking."

Niagaras

"Is this Chris Hoffmann?"

"Yes it is."

"Your name was on a list to call with 40 other guys. Dave Lee is dead. They found him in the bathtub with the barrel of an assault rifle in his mouth."

We were silent for a moment. The guy on the other end of the phone—I never got his name—asked if I could help track down someone on the list. Before we hung up, I asked if there was anything else I should know.

"Yes," he said. "At the top of the list of names was scribbled a single sentence: 'Nobody knows how sad I am.'"

I hung up the phone, turned to walk into the dining room, but only made it three steps. I keeled over on all fours, overtaken with convulsive grief. I couldn't stop—the kind of sobbing where your mouth just gets stuck open, your abdominal muscles contract uncontrollably, and no sound comes out. My daughter came running in. She and my wife looked at me from a distance, not knowing what to do.

Every time I saw Dave, he made me feel like a million dollars. He was an entertainer, a lover of life, and a force to be reckoned with. I recognized early in our friendship that we shared a similar sense of lust for being alive. I'd never been better understood or had my outlook on life captured quite so eloquently by a man, before or since.

I first met Dave on the set of an independent film. I was doing the soundtrack. He was an aspiring screenwriter at the time. Over the years, I watched him get closer and closer to his dream. He boasted he was going all the way and didn't have a plan B. To make cash, he did cold calling for the Yellow Pages. I can't imagine what those over-the-top, Dave-style calls might have been like, but apparently he was good at it.

He would mail me 10-page letters sometimes, each one a big fat bread loaf of a read. Here's a sample of the last letter he wrote after a phone call in which we kicked around the meaning of life:

Adventure just for the.... sake of adventure? Doing shit just.... to prove we're not afraid?

My reaction & thinking in regard to such thinking?

Is: right on, brother. Life is short. And right on.

It was refreshing to hear somebody say such --- in its simplest, straight-up form. There are all kinds of reasons to pursue variety, experience, adventure. To push the envelope (from one side of the desk to the other with, say, the nub of an old golf pencil). To bring on the most powerful drug in the world (adrenaline).

To personally 'stage' and set up unique Niagaras of honest to God stimulation --- and to live actual, new realities, and outcomes.

To me, that sounds about right.

I think we spend too much time in our lives mired in the stressful, time consuming calculus of 'what adventure is right for us?'

.... when life is short.

I don't think 'what' adventure is nearly so important as 'that' there be adventure.

Because, among other things, there's always that one, beautiful, altogether reliable living-formulation to fall back on: One Thing Leads To Another.

I fuckin' love (and hate) that formulation, that fact, that reality.

I hate it because if you're prone to obsessive pursuit, as I am, one thing will, inevitably, and often damnably, lead to another. And another. And before long, you've burned yourself down, and out... without 'getting there.'

But by and large, it's a beautiful, and damned refreshing thing to be reminded of.

Dave Lee – 2008

The last time I visited him, he said he'd be waiting at LAX between Terminals 2 and 3. There wasn't much traffic, so I walked back and forth between the terminals looking for him in the sweltering afternoon sun. I kept passing a beat-up Volvo station wagon with some creepy-looking, unshaven dude napping in the front seat, windows down, head back with a wet towel on his forehead. I eventually walked up to the window.

"Dave?"

He snapped his head up, launching the towel onto the dashboard.

"Hoff-Bräu!" he yelled back.

We were planning to go out that night. At the last minute, he said, "Let's go see *Last Tango in Paris* at this little theatre that sells drinks. I'll get us a date." He went over to the big six-foot wide mirror in his living room. Tucked in the frame, all across the bottom, was a row of actress business card heads shots. He scanned down the row of faces and pulled one out.

"Let's call Sally."

Just looking at all those business cards made me wonder why Dave would have them displayed like that. Did he actually have all these women in play? I never asked.

Next thing I knew, we were pulling up in front of Sally's cute apartment building. She piled in, and I immediately liked her—fun, witty, vibrant, and silly. We roared off to the movie.

Dave was always seemingly at ease with women. There was a confident "dude's dude" way he interacted with women that made it so fun. I was 15 years into a marriage, and really had no idea how to hang with single women. Once Dave showed me how it was done, I was an awesome wingman—together we'd keep women rolling with laughter. I felt alive and free, attractive and smart, things I rarely felt in my home life.

Being the middle of the week, the theatre was totally empty. We took three seats at the center of one aisle, Sally in the middle. Even though I was married, I found myself on full flirtation alert. Not just touching lightly, but intellectually challenging her every chance I got. Dave was a master at filling the air with funny, light conversation. He had her falling into the aisles with one-liners, one after another. Whoever was in the projection booth must have been laughing, too.

During the controversial anal sex scene, our conversation tapered off. We became quiet. There's nothing like watching a man smear a stick of butter on a woman's ass before entering her to bond three people together as if they actually shared a potent physical experience together.

Afterwards, we went and played pool a block from Dave's apartment. The flirting continued. Dave was a guy who would get so much going for himself, and then blow it at the last minute. Like me, he had a deep insecurity, and a dark lack of self-worth. However, he was able to create a wildly entertaining persona that drew people to him. Problem was, he couldn't turn it off when someone just wanted to hear "the real Dave" speak.

Watching Dave overcompensate for his insecurity, I started thinking about how my own lack of self-worth was impacting my life. I wanted intimacy, but I didn't know how to get out of my own head and ego long enough to be my real self either.

As we walked back to his apartment, Dave pulled me aside.

"I need you to get lost for a few hours," he said. "You know, get a coffee or something."

Sally overheard and yelled back to Dave, "Wait, we're all together tonight." I tried to whisper to Dave, "Dude, what are you doing, man? We could all go in, and, you know, light some candles, have an awesome threesome." Dave was adamant—he wanted to ask her up by himself. By this time, Sally was getting annoyed. Finally, she became exasperated, and in her frustration said, "Just take me home, Dave."

Dave told me of another time he blew it, a few years earlier, with a CNN journalist. They met at a party, and kept an email conversation going for months into her assignment in Turkey. He would spend days crafting her funny, thoughtful letters, and then he'd go back through and actually add typos and grammar mistakes to make it look like he'd just pounded it out in one sitting. He said she wrote that she was falling in love with his mind and couldn't wait to see him. After she got back she only saw him a few times, and dumped him. He never said why.

On the last morning of my visit, the Los Angeles heat beating against the windows, Dave and I wandered around his apartment with coffee, bumping into each other in his small galley kitchen. We finally settled into the two big overstuffed chairs that faced each other in the living room. His shirtless athletic body was slouching, and I couldn't help admiring how fabulously fit a man he was. At his core, he was kind of a jock. No matter which city he moved to, he would always find some dudes for games of pickup basketball.

There was a peace hanging in the air that morning. Dave wasn't filling it with stories or chatter, just cradling his cup of warm coffee, and looking out the open window. Outside, sparrows proclaimed the day like a Disney soundtrack. I suddenly felt all his struggle to be a screenwriter, all the schmoozing, cocktail parties, the pitches, the waiting. I knew what it took to be a creative person, to really live it, but unlike him, I always had some other path I could take. For Dave, that wasn't an option.

The morning light through the window fell across his lap in a way that highlighted the bulge in his pajamas. A confusing whisper of an urge came over me to go kneel in front of him and take his cock in my mouth. I had never even thought of doing such a thing, but was immediately aware of the immense chasm between thinking it, and actually *doing* it.

In the gripping confusion of that moment, the idea of putting his cock in my mouth seemed no more radical than actually using *words to just tell him* how I felt; to offer an honest reflection of how I truly saw him, how I felt his emptiness just like mine, and how much I admired him. What would he have done with that information? Would he even have wanted to know that I loved who he was? I realized I was at a complete loss on how to actually reach him. Like so many men, I was stuck in a stalemate, paralyzed from stating the truth of our emotional isolation.

I profoundly regret not having the awareness at the time to have grabbed the "real Dave" by the scruff of the neck to drag him out of the desperate confines of his Hollywood bravado. It honestly devastates me to this day that he didn't stick around. I would love to know him now.

A few months after his death, I bought a gilded picture frame, printed my best photo of Dave with his big smile, and framed it with the following words printed above it:

David Robert Lee, March 6, 1961 – February 1, 2008

Dave, I loved you, man...
sorry the demons in your head got the best of you...

I didn't know how big a place you held in my heart
until you tore it out.

I wish the world we all live in was closer
to the one you imagined.

You would have always been my best friend...

Then I built a bonfire, set the framed photo gently in the middle, and watched it burn.

A Father's Quiet Rage

Like me, my dad grew up building things. I remember old photos of him as a 10-year-old, building a little driftwood dock out into the lake. Or from his 20s, standing next to a mahogany wood speedboat he built in his mother's back yard. He was a straight-talking, honest man who never outwardly manipulated anyone into doing anything.

Being self-made, he didn't believe in college—it was never even talked about in our home. He'd worked in a hardware store before joining the Navy toward the end of WWII. When the war ended, he began his career as a mechanical engineer in the Detroit auto industry, and worked his way up. As he moved through his life, I'm convinced he didn't believe professional or "elite" people would accept him. My mom, who had a fun group of professional creative friends, would ask him to go to a party once in a while, but he was just too intimidated by the comradery. As he aged, his political views leaned increasingly right wing as he isolated himself from those he continued to believe would not include him.

During his 40s, my dad was laid-off for a year during a recession. My mom was working, so he purposefully stayed home and fixed up the house. He didn't even look for work. Being an engineer, he spent months building a good size model sailboat in the back rec room. I had been admiring his daily progress, especially the paint job, when one day I came home from school to find it smashed into little pieces all over his work table. After a few days the work table was cleared off, folded up, and put away. A few weeks later he found a job. No one in our family ever said a word about it.

I am now convinced that behind my dad's mask of dependability and integrity was a passive rage of anger. He endured a traumatic childhood. His brother died from influenza at age 12, and his successful father died as my dad turned 17. His father's death forced his mother to sell their big house on Grand Boulevard in Detroit and move to a small house in a working class neighborhood. She took a job keeping books at an auto body shop, where she stayed for 30 years.

My dad never talked about or displayed emotions. In fact, anytime he showed emotions, it scared me. When I got in trouble as a kid, I remember him calmly asking me whether I wanted "the switch or the belt" for my spanking. In my teens, after fighting with my brother, my father grabbed me by the front of my jacket, lifted me off the ground, and threw me against the coat rack. He then told me never to fight with my brother again. I never did.

I believe, like so many men, my dad was frustrated because the very wall he built around himself to protect his ego invariably isolated him. His self-righteousness gave him a false sense of power and control. Instead of being more resilient, or having compassion for someone else's experience, he just railed against those in power on the outside.

He was proud of his work, but since he didn't think people would include him, he judged those he worked for as corrupt, immoral, or basically not good enough. There were very few people he admired, and if he did, it always came with an asterisk. He wanted things to be organized—everything in his woodshop and in his life had a place and a function—but that very need for order was what limited his freedom.

The frustration women feel with engineers—which sometimes builds to a feather-spitting, blistering tirade—is not "Are you listening to me?" but more honestly, "Do you even know YOURSELF?"

I can remember my mom screaming at my dad, even throwing things across the room to receive not much more of a reaction than, "I'll talk to you when you calm down." It was tough to watch. I'm not sure my mom really knew what she wanted from him. Just once, could he have at least stood up from in front of the TV and walked over to hold her?

Knowing what I know now, this is what I wish I'd shared with my dad, if he could have heard it: the love we show to others is the love we first show to ourselves. It starts by taking time to really know ourselves, and to discover where our judgments limit other people's freedom. It's about knowing where we impose our values on others, and how this imposition limits our ability to see the beauty in *them*.

What are we engineers afraid of? Why all the rules and control over the box we stand in? Why is the mystery of life so scary to comprehend? Why are we so afraid of what people will think of our uniqueness that we establish norms that force us to be homogenous? Why do we create an artificial "other class of people" or "other class of art" only for the sole purpose of identifying them as *not us*?

Why can't we as engineers, with all our inventiveness, with our abilities to process complex data, start to create a world that is designed at its core to break down the barriers that separate us? Can't we come to love the very people we rail against—the ones we use to medicate our self-loathing?

☼

My dad's pent-up rage, while having appeared mild on the outside, is essentially the same anger that drives many men to commit acts of violence. From storming out of a job, to kicking the door open on the way out of an estranged girlfriend's house, to shooting someone six times in the chest "just because it felt good," anger screams for control over the madness.

Through the years, I could feel my dad's rage building in me. I could see its effect on our entire family, and was determined to avoid inheriting his same box of desperation and isolation. In small intentional steps of rebellion, I began testing the status quo and unspoken rules of conformity. Eventually, I found the courage to physically act out against the rigidity by accessing a more primal part of myself. To do this, I experimented with building and wearing archetypal costumes, dancing, and going to sexuality awareness classes. Unlike my father, I DID want to thrive in the outside world and have a good home life. I came to believe the RYNO bike was my "best shot" at following my passions—something that would allow me to feel my full potential, and simultaneously fulfill my role as provider for my family.

After smashing my face and hands, what seemed like a fun new product idea suddenly became dangerous. It was clear to me that going down the RYNO path, and having this "normal life" as well, was going to be difficult. I saw that the bike demanded some honest answers I hadn't even thought of until I was too broken to do anything but sit around and think. Why had I wanted to do this in the first place? Why was this particular passion no longer welcome at my house? How would I continue? What else should I be feeding if I was going to stop feeding my ego?

Sitting with all that, I realized I was on the same ego-possessed path as Dave Lee. It scared the hell out of me. I was literally riding my version of Dave's ego-driven, attention-getting Hollywood screenwriting career. When I went out on the RYNO, I felt like I was riding spread eagle into a coliseum of cheering fans. It was such a seductive feeling. I was developing this product out of a drive to outdo everything and everyone. But at what cost? It was my "Niagara," and now it was parked in a heap in my backyard studio.

Encounter with a Tantrika

During this period of reckoning I developed a stinging in my prostate like being stabbed in the groin with a hot icepick all day, every day. I'm telling you, it sure is difficult to hold a quiet, calm conversation with an icepick in your ass.

For a year, I went to doctors and urologists, and even had one of the doctors run a foot-long, stainless steel tube up my urethra only to tell me he didn't "see anything abnormal."

I gave up on Western medicine and started visiting wellness clinics. This is where I found a course listing on a bulletin board that led me to attend a Sacred Sexuality workshop.

It was a gender-balanced event in a sunlit meeting room, 20 or so people getting together monthly to explore and understand their sexuality in a safe, fully-clothed setting. People were arranged in concentric circles—men faced out, women across from each man facing in. Each couple was encouraged by a facilitator to repeat a small statement to one another, something like, "Say a word to the person across from you that reminds you of the way they feel to you," or "Say their name three times with the last time like you really love them."

At the end of each exchange, the facilitator rang a small bell to signal the women to move one position over to sit across from a new male partner. These meetings were calming and fun, but what I realized was even though I thought I was relatively nonjudgmental, my judgement was actually significantly alive. I would sit across from someone only to find myself judging them by their clothes, their hair, their teeth, then tuck them neatly into a category that was "not like me." After each new encounter, by getting to know them, I discovered I was always completely wrong—they were never who I originally thought they were.

After enough of these meetings, I began to realize just how woven into my psyche this judgement was.

Knowing there were emotional survival tools in play, it still took a very conscious effort to dismantle this ugly habituated mannerism. As I found myself becoming more skillful at opening up to a wider variety of people, the knee-jerk reaction of judgment began to fade. As a result, the biggest unexpected surprise was I stopped judging myself so harshly. I found the same opening of inclusion I shared with others allowed my own inner critic to soften. I began to try new things, and experiment with types of expression I would never have attempted before.

It was at one of these Sacred Sexual Workshops where I met Magdalena, the Tantrika. The term was new to me. As I discovered, Tantrika can be defined in many ways: a practitioner of powerful ritual acts of body, mind, and spirit; or a sacred whore; or, as she described herself, a sex therapist who doesn't do much talking.

She was a slight woman with kind eyes, and a bit older. She wore a colorful top over some tights, with a tribal looking neck piece adorned with colorful beads and metal work. Following through with the exercise, we exchanged our assigned words.

"I respect your place on this planet," I said in a gracious and affirming way.

When she spoke the same words back to me, it was as if they came right out of her soft, piercing eyes. As those spirit-infused words lingered, I took them deep into my heart. I felt a little light turn on in me. Something was coming alive.

When the workshop was over, I approached Magdalena and shared that something about her resonated with me. Once I understood what she did for a living, it wasn't long before my prostate issue came up. She said she had proven approaches that worked with men like me, and offered her card.

I continued to try other homeopathic remedies to manage my prostate pain, and almost starved myself on rice and beans to "cleanse my system." Even with my wife's approval, it still took me six months to muster the courage to call Magdalena.

A week after I finally made an appointment, I walked in the front door of a rustic three-story house. Magdalena, wearing a light summer dress, greeted me with a warm smile. I filled out a form with language about consent, something about sexual healing, her fee, and other disclaimers.

She led me upstairs into a large room lit with candles and adorned with wispy drapes. There was incense, Middle Eastern art, a colorful futon, and soft ethereal music playing. For the first half hour, we sat on floor pillows. She asked me about myself, revisited why I was here, and what I wanted to accomplish. After this, she agreed the best approach would be a therapeutic prostate massage.

She extended her small hand to invite me to stand up, and pointed to a sarong draped across the bed.

"I want you to remove all of your clothes," she said softly, "wrap the sarong around your waist, and lie face up with your head on the pile of pillows against the wall."

She left the room as I prepared. When she returned, she was wearing little more than a sarong—the hint of a G-string showed through its thin fabric. She slowly climbed toward me, and sat between my widened legs. She said she would ask permission to touch me in different ways during our time together.

"You're the client, Chris," she went on, her voice soft and affirming, full of compassion. "That means you're the recipient of my care." She made it clear I shouldn't touch her with my hands, and wasn't to expect our encounter to involve me directing any energy toward her. I was to receive and not generate.

Magdalena began the session by lightly running her fingertips up and around my torso. She gently extended my arms out to the side, and placed them softly on pillows. She ran her fingers down my arms, then wisped lightly off my hands as if casting away some form of dust.

She moved down around my waist, then my legs, repeating the casting-off motion with my feet. Then she slowly settled back in between my legs and gazed down at my flaccid cock.

"May I touch you there?" she asked. I agreed. She dipped her fingers in a bowl of warm oil, brought them into contact with my cock, and with a gliding sensation started massaging the length of my shaft. She did so in a calm, loving, and attentive way that was entirely new to me.

In my 20s, the encounters between women and my cock consisted mostly of them pulling on it to get it hard. In married life, if it wasn't ready for sex, I used my own hand to wake it up in a hurried stroking rhythm. As for having my cock sucked, I didn't really enjoy the act—it was too stressful. *Was she getting tired?* I'd catch myself thinking. *Was I ever going to come? What if I can't get hard at all?*

In contrast, this introduction to my experience with Magdalena was deeply pleasurable, therapeutic, and unattached to any outcome. It felt like she was in perfect harmony with my body. It still took me a while to relax enough to find my erection. Her hand motions went on for quite a while, coaxing me into a languid, relaxing, dreamy state. I felt exquisitely seen and accepted. Even the way my breath moved through my lungs felt relaxed and open. In that state, my hard cock was the center of a new awareness of pleasure. It was no longer the center of fear, but a newfound confidence and connection to a part of myself I had never really known. I wanted to get to know my cock in this new way.

The relaxed state of my hard cock took on a unique quality, almost like it had its own self-awareness. The touch Magdalena maintained called my cock forward into a powerful awakening.

At one point she leaned forward and took the length of my cock in her flat palms—one hand on each side as if in prayer. She started taking deep breaths, and exhaled like she was fogging a mirror, her warm breath only an inch away. Each time she moved up to the head of my cock, I fantasized about what it would feel like to have her lips kiss the head of it—to feel that exotic connection.

With my arms stretched out to the sides, I gripped the edge of the mattress tightly to resist the desire to run my fingers through her hair. I knew my place in this—do not disrupt where she was taking me; let go of the need to generate.

She opened her eyes, and ran her gathered fingertips in one last slow motion down the length of my cock, then wisped them out across my pelvis.

"I'm going to place my fingers inside you now," she explained, "to press on your prostate. I'm asking you to listen to my instructions carefully as we move through different waves of treatment. You will feel some pain as we breathe into the experience."

She asked me to take a deep breath, then let it out. As I exhaled, she slid one finger into me, up to the first knuckle. The music in the room was suddenly much more noticeable. I tried to relax, but even one finger inside my rectal canal was a lot to endure.

"Take another breath," she directed, "then let it out." She slid her finger decisively deeper. A long, low groan leaked out of my throat. She slowly slid her finger out and asked me to breathe in and out again. She then asked me to breathe in, and slid her finger deeper. She hooked her finger, and started to apply pressure on my prostate. My groan took on a throaty resonance.

"Breathe," she said.

Using muscles I'd never felt, I found a way to relax and open a bit. She advanced, then lingered while I managed the uncomfortable pressure. I repositioned myself a few times to get the angle right. Each time she went deeper and pressed harder. She wasn't talking now, just breathing with me to keep me engaged with my breath. The pain grew more intense, and more frightening—at times I thought I was about to hyperventilate. Was this the wall to push through, or was it still yet to come? She took her time, repeating this rhythm of relaxing, then applying more pressure.

She repositioned herself on her knees, and indicated she was going to apply even more pressure. She said fluid may come out of my "lingam," which was Tantrika speak for cock. She told me not to worry.

Her sarong fell down around her waist. Her breasts swayed in rhythm with her muscular movements as she manipulated my pelvis. The soft music became an annoying distraction.

She had two fingers inside me now, and was almost lifting my pelvis off the futon. My prostate was at the center of all my physical awareness. Then three fingers were inside me, and my legs were up on her shoulders. Through the haze of searing pain, I somehow had broken through that fiery state into total surrender. On the other side, the pain had vanished. It was completely surreal—not even a lingering rawness of something that still needed more time to heal.

I almost began to weep from the relief.

Magdalena sweetly and skillfully wound me down to a quiet state of being. I felt myself become a little self-conscious at how exposed I was. She put her hand on my thigh and held it there, as if she knew what I was thinking. Here was a woman, a paid professional, acting as my advocate to heal me from my pain. She'd created a sensual encounter with a focus on waking my body up through tactile engagement, then leading me through an intense treatment that had deep, therapeutic value.

"Stay still as long as you'd like," she whispered, then slipped out of the room.

As I lay back, the relaxation was like sliding down into a warm bath—a stark contrast to the pain I'd been living with. I almost fell asleep right there. The air filled my lungs effortlessly and drifted out like little waves lapping on a beach. So much presence in my body all of a sudden—just to be in a body that felt at peace and alive was such a newfound joy.

There are challenges we simply can't intellectualize our way out of. For me to feel my challenges, I usually hammered or pounded them out—the house, the bike, my life. Give me tools and a project, and my mind will find peace. Magdalena showed me another choice: to actively and deliberately put myself in a position where I could receive. To surrender, and not in a "feel-good, blissed out" way, but as purposeful act of self-preservation.

As a man, you can't do this kind of work—put yourself in a position of vulnerability—and not be ready to die a little. It's hard to discover this level of trust, but once we learn to accept new possibilities, people like Magdalena will appear around us to help—as long as we're willing to find them.

I thanked Magdalena, and told her I felt inspired and relieved. She'd pointed a symbolic flashlight down a long path I had never seen before, and gave me the courage to start walking.

And then the sadness hit me.

☼

She stood in front of me as I was about to leave. She sensed it, and asked if I was okay. I admitted I wasn't. I didn't know how to inspire or create this type of healing in my marriage. I felt trapped in a relationship dynamic I had created and allowed to exist, and was losing the desire to try and change things.

"If you want to discover how sad you are," she said, "find a quiet place at home when everyone is gone. Sit with your forehead in your hands, and imagine falling down a well. Your sadness is proportional to how far and fast you fall."

A few days later, my wife and daughter were out shopping. I'd thought about Magdalena's challenge, but was terrified to try it. I paced the living room, then finally sat down in front of our fireplace. A long exhale left me. I felt defeated and alone. I placed my forehead in my hands and started falling . . . and falling . . . and falling . . . until I accelerated into a free fall. In the past, I would have made myself stop. This time, I let it all go.

There was no bottom.

I had no idea I was hiding so skillfully behind a false sense of identity. The realization of what our house represented, and what it required of me to sustain it, became crystal clear. I was using my ability to create physical structures—house, bike . . . the hammer, the project—as a way to impose myself on the world around me. The house I'd spent a decade restoring was supposed to create an ideal family. It didn't happen.

Now the bike was supposed to make me rich and famous, but it had its own agenda. I was becoming bitter and controlling, flailing in my attempts to just come out and say what wasn't working in my marriage. I wasn't leading or modeling a path forward—I was just complaining about the road I was on.

I mumbled into my hands something about *this is my life,* but even then I knew I was too scared to confidently claim those words for myself.

Who did I think I was anyway, to actually stand up for what I wanted?

After my descent into this well of sadness, I'd spend another year floundering around with half-baked attempts at salvaging my marriage before I realized I no longer wanted to fix any of it.

The Box I Built

Jean and I were married for 20 years. Peek in our windows, and you'd say everything looked great—the cooking, the house, our daughter, the dog. We rarely disagreed, and we got a lot done. Years went by in relative compatibility. But as I started to wake up, I realized the honeymoon love we'd shared years earlier hadn't evolved into a mature adult partnership. Jean seemed to be fine with things, but I wanted a deeper sense of connection—something that felt sexy. Instead of working toward a shared goal, we started hiding from it—and from ourselves.

Once the main floor restoration was done, we moved into our gorgeous bedroom. Our window looked out to a wonderful view of grapevines wrapping around the porch. For me, the room was an amazing oasis—just add candles, and it could be instant romance. For Jean, the room needed a TV. Within a few weeks, I came home to see a monolith-sized set atop the dresser at the foot of our bed.

All families fall into rhythms, for better or worse. Even though I didn't want the TV in our bedroom, it wasn't long before she and I found ourselves in front of it. We'd invite our daughter into our room, then we'd all pile together and watch movies and shows—a nice family vibe. But the friction eventually started to burn inside of me. Soon it triggered thoughts of my dad: as a kid, I had to compete with TV for his attention; now I was doing the same thing for Jean's.

Whenever Lauren would have a party, we'd move the TV to the living room so she and her friends could play video games. With the TV gone, I could feel our bedroom breathe. I would ask Jean if we could keep it out of the room for good, and she would argue that there wasn't any other place for it. Eventually, I would give up and dutifully carry it back into our room.

Apart from these struggles, Jean and I had created a beautiful home together. She was the art director; I was the builder. When we finished restoring the dining room, our family would sit down for a candlelit dinner almost every night. We'd talk about Lauren's day at school, or I would talk about the office—normal, traditional stuff, completely devoid of vibrancy.

It's funny, sort of, how we subconsciously recreate familiarity. I'd essentially married my dad—since I didn't know how to "do emotions," as the saying went, I'd found a woman who didn't expect a lot of them from me. At the same time, the way I viewed Jean as a woman was similar to how I related to my mother—constantly trying to be sensitive to her anxiety, waiting for it be my fault, then seeking to "fix it." To fill my desire to be a "good husband," I unwittingly used a classic pleaser dynamic to keep Jean happy, usually at my own expense.

I began to see that the whole thing was artifice or scenery. I'd been bitching to my close friends about "playing an assigned role," and blaming the whole thing on Jean. In truth, I was the one who'd built the box I was railing against. And I was the one forcing myself to stand inside of it.

First Date in Eighteen Years

Toward the end of our marriage, as my jaw and hands recovered from the accident, I negotiated something called "sanctioned sexual encounters." It was an idea that sort of fell out of my mouth as it hung open while Jean and I were on the couch sharing a joint.

"Do you ever want to have sex with me again?" I asked her.

She paused, took a nice drag, and slowly let the smoke out.

"Not really," she sighed. "I'm not even sure I like cocks anymore."

It hurt to hear, but I respected her honesty. Still, my chest collapsed a little at her abruptness.

"You mind if I find a girlfriend then?" I was surprised by how easily the question came. "Physical intimacy is kind of important to me."

A few days later I cycled back to the topic. I never thought something like having a girlfriend was even an option, so I hadn't been thinking much about it. Now, I wanted us both to look it in the eye. I asked her point-blank what she thought about me actually seeing someone. She seemed exceptionally complacent about it—a little too complacent, like she figured it would never happen because of how shut down I was with her. I appreciated her willingness to outsource our intimacy, but was sad that she didn't want to fight to keep sexually investing in our relationship.

※

Rose was an unlikely choice. The first time I saw her was at a Sacred Sexuality workshop. Laying eyes on her tattooed, athletic body, I was immediately intimidated. Not just a few tattoos—I'm talking full-on arm cuffs, and her legs, chest, and back were completely covered. On top of that, her hair was a wild mat of twisted dreadlocks. She reminded me of the girls I'd seen on SuicideGirls.com, a website that fascinated me as I surfed porn late at night. Granted, I'd hung out with a lot of edgy looking women in my punk days back in Detroit, but I was a lot older now, and wasn't sure what I'd even say to a woman so radically expressed.

I ran into Rose again at a different workshop. We were paired together, which allowed us to get to know one another a bit. We chatted more at the potluck afterward. I found out she was a yoga teacher, and also taught self-defense classes to women. She had a feisty edge to the way she talked, and I gave it right back to her. She seemed to genuinely take a liking to me. I wanted to ask her for her number, then thought about what Dave Lee would have done. He had a way of just saying shit and following it with a disarming grin. So I let the conversation stall, looked her in the eyes, and said, "Do you want to give me your number?" She looked back at me and said, "I'm not sure, but if you ask for it, I might." I huffed a laugh, and did just that.

I called her a few days later.

Rose said she needed to buy a Christmas present for her mom, and was thinking of a cordless drill. She asked if I could meet her at Home Depot to help her pick one out. "Then we could take it from there," she offered. I agreed to meet her the next day.

As planned, I stood outside under the big orange entrance sign scanning for her arrival. With the smell of freshly milled two-by-fours wafting through the air, the beeping sound of a forklift backing up, and dudes dressed in work clothes shuffling by, I felt totally in my element—secure and manly.

I almost missed her crossing toward the other entrance. I yelled, and she shifted gears toward me. She walked like a little drill sergeant—strutting confidently, a woman who knew herself and what she was doing. I started imagining what an erotic encounter with her might be like—it kind of scared me.

After a brief hug, I said I liked her new spikey haircut. She thanked me, and explained that last night, in a fit of wanting to change her life, she cut off her dreadlocks with a dull pair of scissors. Then she explained that she hadn't figured out what hairstyle she wanted quite yet. I relaxed a bit hearing her say that. She clearly was NOT a perfectionist, and didn't give a fuck what people thought of her hair—certainly not me. It made her even more attractive and sexy—such a freeing contrast to Jean, who meticulously art-directed *everything*.

Walking the aisles, Rose fired off all kinds of hardware questions—total bliss for any engineer. Her attention to my answers made me feel important. She walked in an engaging rhythm that sort of pulled me along, a coaxing challenge to keep up with her stride. I kept feeling like I wanted to wrestle with her. I finally gave her shoulder a teasing and impulsive shove. She shoved right back and dropped into a little *let's play* crouch, taunting me to wonder what it would be like to pin her down and feel the resistance of her tight yoga body.

We finally arrived at the place where I come to worship—the tool section. A few specific questions later, we nailed the drill purchase, then wandered out into the adjoining mall.

We sat down on a wooden park bench by an empty fountain. Twenty-five years ago, I would have entered into my *trying to impress a woman with my wit* torrent. This was different. I was a little wiser and clear-headed now. I had a genuine interest in where she was in her life, and what she wanted. The compassion between us took me by surprise. I'd been so angry and unfulfilled at home. Rose's genuine curiosity allowed me to drop into a version of myself I hardly knew. I liked this guy.

My breathing slowed way down, started coming from a deeper part of my lungs. I put my weight against her, and she tipped her head to touch mine. We sat like that for what felt like an hour until a loudspeaker voice startled us back to reality—the mall was closing soon.

Outside, I watched her disappear into the sea of parked cars with her new drill. The sun was setting. We made plans to see each other again. I did all I could to not project too far into that future.

The next morning, I mustered the courage to tell Jean about Rose, even offered to introduce her at some point. There was a pause, then Jean said she was still okay with our agreement. Great, I thought. Then I imagined the three of us sitting in a coffee shop together—that vision gave my asshole a serious pucker.

☼

I called Rose a few days later with a plan to go on a long hike with a packed lunch.

"Or, you could just come over to my house," she said coyly.

I was so focused on the idea of the hike that I almost didn't register what she was saying.

"Oh, your place sounds much quieter," I finally stammered.

Two days later, I parked in front of her house and started toward the door. I had absolutely no idea what I was doing. Who did I think I was? She couldn't really be into me, a middle-aged married guy. It made no sense. I had no plan, no flowers, no bottle of wine—nothing. Each step brought me closer to a great unknown. At one point, I stopped cold in her front yard. As I struggled with my approach, I finally snapped-to, and said to myself, "I'm going in BIG."

She opened the door slowly and smiled. I took a deep breath and strutted into the middle of her tiny living room.

"What do you want to do?" she asked. "Sit on the couch and talk? Maybe share an orange?"

"I want to get BUSY," I announced. Rose perked up.

"Great!"

Her reply almost knocked me over.

"What do you want to do?" she asked.

"I want to go into your bedroom and slowly peel your clothes off."

"Awesome."

To my surprise, she spun around and disappeared down the hallway. I started to follow, then realized *Fuck—18 years since I'd been to a woman's house, what was I supposed to do with all this?*

She stood at the foot of her bed and faced me. I confidently stepped forward, gripped the bottom of her spaghetti strap top, and slowly pulled it over her head—her perfect *real, live tits* beamed back at me. After I flicked her shirt off, she continued to hold her arms up over her head. I gently ran my fingertips from her wrists down to her shoulder blades, past the sides of her narrow ribcage, gliding down over an illustrated storybook of tattoos. The words "Your honesty is like a kiss on my lips" were inked arching from one hip bone to the other.

I unbuckled her jeans and gave them a quick tug.

"Sit down on the edge of the bed," I commanded.

"Yes, sir!" she exclaimed.

Once her legs were free, she unfolded them like a soft pair of wings, wide apart in a welcoming invitation. To my surprise, a big, carnival barker energy came over me.

"Look at that pussy, ladies and gentlemen," I started to yell. "Will somebody PLEASE shine a light down on that gorgeous pussy?"

Rose cracked a wide smile. I could handle this. I drifted down slowly and slid my hands around her waist, then lowered my tongue flat onto her blonde muff.

I could never be this free with Jean. I was always the one to initiate. After making love, she would often say things like she *forgot how good it was*, or how we should *try to do this more often*, but her interest would always fade.

As the tongue lashing continued, Rose squealed, writhed, arched her back, and finally reached down and pulled me up to join her. We were lost in a wonderland of pleasure. She rolled on top of me. I smacked her ass as she reached into her nightstand to grab lube. I could see her drawer was neatly arranged with glass dildos, a leather flogger, a basket of condoms, and a stack of folded hand towels. This woman's sexuality was clearly a priority—all her toys were neatly organized and tooled-up for pleasure. *Fuck,* I thought, *so this is what a touch of liberation tastes like.*

Suddenly, my brain kicked back online. Shouldn't we have had a "safe sex" conversation? Weren't things moving a little *too fast*? Was I pleasing her the right way? All this thinking caused me to hesitate. I felt flooded and didn't know what to do next. The momentum of our romp suddenly stumbled to a stop.

Rose sensed the change in energy, but was kind about it. She kissed me.

"You mind if I get myself off?" she asked gently.

"Go for it," I said.

She reached between the bed and the wall to pull out what looked like a medium-sized baseball bat—pink with a round knob on one end, a fat white power cord on the other.

She clicked it to the on position, held the soft bulbous head firmly against her clit, and started to go off somewhere mystical. Her chest heaved and turned bright red. Her breathing erupted into the sound of wind howling through the forest.

I stayed in the room but drifted off into my own thoughts. Years ago, another lifetime even, I ended up at a peep show in Flint, Michigan, after one of our punk rock gigs. Sitting alone in a room the size of a phone booth, I put a quarter in the slot. A rollup curtain lifted. On the other side of the glass, a nude woman undulated on the floor to the sound of cheesy porn music.

I held my cock through my jeans, but I wasn't interested in getting off. What I felt instead was a sense of admiration for the woman. I could sense her openness. She lingered in the direction of each man who stared from separate windows, shared with them what looked like a warm smile, then moved to the next. Our eyes met just as she was ramping up her orgasm. In that moment, she modeled a quality of eroticism that resonated closer to the surface than anything I even knew existed. An erotic carrier frequency connected us, traveled back and forth through my window. Then she closed her eyes, and drifted off somewhere deep into her own orgasmic pleasure.

I twisted Rose's nipples, gripped her heaving breasts as the rushing air filled her lungs deeper and deeper. Her orgasm started with a muffled moan, then a scream built up and out of her, finally resolving into a yelling convulsion. I was sure the neighbors were going to hear her. What a thing to witness—a beautiful woman claiming her total erotic autonomy and expression.

Once she settled, she looked at me sideways, pleasure-drunk.

"Well, THAT felt good," she gasped.

I went back to her place five times over the next few months. I wasn't clear on what I wanted from our encounters, so I didn't invest too heavily in what could or should happen. Sometimes we just talked on her couch. Other times, I'd fix a few things for her. Regardless, we would always find ourselves in one form or another of erotic play. She was always kind, sweet, and patient. I loved licking her pussy, but still hadn't found my way to having intercourse with her.

During each drive to Rose's, I'd wonder about what would happen this time. What improvisation would we embark on? What silly act of kindness would befall one of us? Then, driving home, I would always feel a bit overwhelmed. I'd start appreciating my calm home life with Jean. The best way I can describe my emotional state: I felt undone and untethered. Something was unraveling, but I couldn't name it. I was oscillating between two worlds—half here, half there.

The last time I visited Rose, I was finally ready to offer my cock to her. That's when she let me know she was going back to a monogamous relationship with her boyfriend. The news came with a lacerating sting, like something being ripped off my body, opening a freshly healed wound.

I puffed a few shallow breaths. We held each other in a warm embrace. I walked out to my car alone and sat there for a few minutes, a bit dizzy, then headed back to the other world.

THUD

In the months after my RYNO accident, I built a new friendship network that was different from any group of friends I'd ever had. No gritty Detroit punk rock edge, no starving New York artist scene, no child-rearing, crunchy granola Portland urbanites. These new friends were wide open, completely present in each moment, and entirely at peace in their skin. Jean was intimidated by them. I joined them at potluck parties, meet-ups, dancing, and late night hot tub soaks. At first, I would ask if Jean wanted to come, but she was never into it. She didn't like that the quiet engineer who used to go with her to art openings in New York was changing.

I spent many long nights staring at the ceiling as Jean slept next to me. I just couldn't imagine a clear scenario that would keep our family intact. We were shut down and sad. Neither of us wanted to find the strength to do anything differently. It seemed like the only path forward was to dismantle the whole house—and the family inside—then put the cash in the bank to keep everyone safe.

I knew if I implemented this plan, I'd wind up living in a small rented room somewhere.

Instead, we decided to try couples therapy again. As part of our plan, Jean and I agreed that I'd call some of my female friends and tell them I wouldn't be around much.

☼

I went out to our backyard studio to start making calls. I sat and stared at the spot where I'd hauled the RYNO after the accident. By now, I'd moved the bike to a friend's machine shop, and cleaned up my work area. A few RYNO sketches still hung on the wall above my workbench, like pictures of old friends you keep around.

My first call was to a woman named Joanne, an artist I had known for a few years. I started telling her that Jean and I were going to try counseling again. She cut in right away.

"Can you hear the sound of your voice?" she asked. "You sound like you're dying. You can't keep doing this and think it's going to be any different."

I told her I didn't think I had the courage to leave. Joanne shot back that she didn't have the courage to keep hearing me complain about it.

"Nice one," I said. I thanked her for the tough love and hung up.

Next was Diane. She was a powerhouse of a woman—clear and honest. Once when I was at her house, she overheard me talking with Jean on the phone. When the call was over, she just stared at me for a long moment.

"What woman would speak to a man in a way that makes him give up his power?" she asked. "Did you hear how high and thin your voice got? Where did your throat go?"

When Diane answered her phone, I could barely find the words to tell her Jean and I were going to try counseling again.

"If you don't get out of there right now," she said, "then I'm coming over with three of my friends to get you."

"You're right," I mumbled. I stood in a marked silence, thanked her, and hung up.

The idea of tough love banged around my brain. It's not something we think of in a community focused on mindfulness. These women—equal turns powerful and graceful, kind, articulate, well-intentioned—decided to cut straight to the heart of things. They were frustrated with me—and for me. And they let that frustration show. Were they soft in their replies? No. Would I have heard them had they been more respectful and honoring of my process? Tough to say.

What I knew was this: as I left the studio and started toward the house, a dimly lit bridge appeared across a deep chasm. I stood in the dark, my head burning from the heat of trying to process what to do. I wasn't just oscillating now—I was breaking down. There was the world of my conventional life: a steady job where I gave my paycheck to Jean and she paid the bills; our mutual friends; our daughter; the house. Then there was the world I was building with these new big-hearted people: we camped together, danced together, and kept track of each other's lives. I could choose one or the other, but they couldn't co-exist.

I stared at that bridge. All I had to do was walk across it and leave all of this behind. But where would I go? I called Sally, another friend who knew my situation.

"Can I sleep at your place tonight?" I asked. "I need to get out of here. I have no idea where to go." There was a long pause. To my relief, she said, "Sure, what time?"

"An hour," I said. Just saying the words conjured both horror and relief—for the first time, I actually had a plan.

With that, a small spotlight came on over the bridge. All I had to do was walk. The fear of my own self-annihilation made my head throb. My chest burned like someone was dragging a rake across my body.

Fuck, what about our daughter? She was 16 now—sweet, respectful, deeply empathic for her age. I always made sure she had a voice when it came to sharing her needs—a stark difference to my own reality as a teenager, when my father's style was to offer his plan, slap a timeline on it, and tell us to go. Was I breaking an unspoken promise to her? Was I more like my father than I wanted to admit? Did Lauren already know I wasn't the man I wanted to be, and couldn't possibly be the father our family needed?

Who was the man I wanted to be? I knew for sure I couldn't find him in this house. But where?

This weight of family bore down onto my shoulders—my daughter's safety and happiness, my wife's survival. How could I do this to them?

The bridge looked inviting, but would it actually take me anywhere? Or would it snap beneath my weight the moment I was half-way across, dropping me into the abyss?

My mind was like a manual transmission with the synchronizers all shot. No matter how hard I jammed the shifter, and no matter what gear I ground, nothing was clicking in to engage. I was a builder. I needed a plan I could implement. As this one started to form, I was still terrified.

A complete and utter void stared back at me.

In my paralyzed stupor I must have relaxed a bit—I finally felt my transmission slip into gear with a confident THUD.

I launched onto that bridge. Then the reality hit me: this life was not serving *any of us*. That gave me the momentum to accelerate, to charge across with enough speed that, even if the bridge gave way, I could still make it to the other side.

I twisted the knob to the back door. It was all I could do to calm my adrenaline and keep from swinging the door right off its hinges.

I coasted into the kitchen like I'd seen a ghost. Jean had just dropped two ice cubes into a gin and tonic. The sound of the ice against the glass normally marked that the day was done, evening was here. But the look on her face as she stared at me said something different.

There's nothing like the four words "we need to talk" to stop two people in their tracks. Jean and I watched each other for a second, then I continued toward the bedroom, passing Lauren, who was doing her homework. Jean followed.

I closed the bedroom door. I felt completely exhausted—back hunched, shoulders bent forward. A long, trembling exhale came out of me.

"I can't do this anymore."

I turned to gather my cell phone charger and some clothes from the dresser.

"Fuck you, asshole," Jean yelled. Funny—in that moment I felt kind of proud of her for accessing something authentic and real.

I bounded toward the living room. Jean followed. Lauren looked up from her homework. Before I had a chance to say something to her, Jean started yelling.

"Say goodbye to your father, Lauren, he's going out the front door!"

I turned away. My pace through the front door was more like running than walking. It was all I could do to shake off the fear of being dragged back. I threw my things onto the passenger seat and put the car in drive.

Everything was crumbling, and I didn't even have the strength to comfort my daughter in that moment.

What kind of man was I?

PART 2:
BUILDER

Early in my engineering career, I realized that by building utilitarian things, I was calibrating my skills to add value to those around me. It was clear that if I built things, I could earn my place in a stable group. I was good at it, enough so that I didn't have to learn much else. As long as I found a group that needed a builder or engineer, I could stay relatively unconscious to other aspects of my life: the parts of me that wanted to create and experience beauty.

Inventor Child

As a boy I built my own toys. My engineer dad always had a woodshop in the basement. He showed me how to use power tools at a young age. Soon I was building small boats to play with on the carpet, little airplanes with twisted rubber bands for springs, even a six-foot-long catapult with slices of a tree trunk for wheels.

When I was 10, I made a doll out of a piece of wood, screw eyes, and some dowels—my own little stick figure with articulated joints, like an avatar. When I would get anxious at home, I'd take it out in the front yard, throw it up in the air as far as I could, then yell at the top of my lungs as if I was the one falling through the sky. This went on for years. It truly was my first experience of building something tangible to elicit a feeling.

When I was 12, my friends and I started playing Civil War games. Of course, I had to build a wooden Gatling machine-gun from broomstick handles mounted on a tripod made from two-by-fours. I literally sawed off a few feet from all the brooms in the house to make the eight gun barrels. My mom was not happy.

In my freshman year in high school metal shop, I machined a replica naval cannon with a 16-inch-long barrel. It went on to win first place in the state industrial arts competition.

Junior year, I built a giant medieval crossbow ballista from a truck leaf spring. It would shoot broomstick-size arrows through a tree. I still didn't know why I was doing this. At parents night, I stood by my giant crossbow in the hallway alongside other kids' shop projects—things like hammers and bird feeders. I derived some satisfaction from the stares of confused parents as they walked past me with my long hair, dressed in a red and gray marching band coat from Goodwill.

Building tree forts throughout my childhood progressed from nailing primitive boards in a tree, to constructing a fully enclosed, two-story swank house with a bay window, complete with a pot-belly stove. The township made the land owner tear it down or pay taxes on it.

Clearly, I was a productive and talented kid, but my parents gave me very little emotional support, and never recognized the unique output of my creative expression. Many times, I would build things just to get my dad's attention. I'd run in to show him before the paint was even dry. He would comment on the craftsmanship, maybe the effort, but not much more.

On Being Invincible

Once I hit high school, my dad made it clear he was done with giving me an allowance. I had to get a job, which was a bitch without a car. My dad would never drive me anywhere. I can remember lots of times walking outside and sticking my thumb to hitchhike to work or wherever I needed to go.

My high school art teacher recommended me to a job helping design and build window displays at the big chain store downtown. I hated it, along with a string of other jobs.

Over the summer before twelfth grade, my dad finally agreed to let me work at his engineering office running blueprints and getting doughnuts. It took me all summer to earn $700 to buy a car. My dad offered to help me choose a model that would be practical transportation, but on a whim I hitchhiked to look at a 1947 vintage Willys Jeep—bright yellow with no top at all, just a roll bar. It had a low set of differential gears so it would only do 55 MPH flat out, but the guy said it would climb a wall. I was so excited I bought it on the spot and drove it home.

My dad was not pleased.

I attended high school in the urban sprawl of Detroit, Michigan. Subdivisions were gobbling up farm fields at a rapid pace. As a result, the school population was a mix of farm kids, jocks, and hippies. The way we partied was to find a remote field or gravel pit, and put out the word. A hundred kids would converge on the location, park their cars on a dirt road, and hike back to crowd around a bonfire away from the cops.

When I bought the jeep, I immediately imagined that it would easily navigate the foot trails back to the field parties. On weekends, I terrorized every back trail, river bed, pasture land and forest I could find with it. I kept a big pair of wire cutters next to my seat because of all the barbwire I kept wrapping around my axle.

The first time I drove up to a bonfire party, all the kids ran screaming—they thought I was the cops. It was so fun to draw that kind of attention. Girls would almost line up to pile in and go for joy rides up and down the hills, and along the edge of the waterhole.

I had no real idea why this was so important to me. I didn't know how to hit on the girls—it was all just a big screaming show. I imagine the other dudes must have thought I was a total asshole for stealing the attention and making it all about me. I even rigged up speakers and an eight-track deck so I could drive up with music blaring. That probably pissed them off even more.

At age 19 I bought a 1968 Chevy Chevelle SS hot rod with a big V8 and flames on it. I drove the shit out of that car, and in the process blew up two engines, tore the gears out of the rear end, and broke the drive shaft. I became so good at fixing that machine I swear I could have taken it apart with my eyes closed. It had a four-eleven Positraction rear end, which made it perfect for burning doughnuts outside every party I went to. There too, I would always find some girl to agree to go for a ride in it, then scare the crap out of her as I did smoking four-wheel drifts around the sweeping corners in the newly poured concrete subdivisions.

Hell yes, I was invincible. I didn't even care what the girl's experience was as she got out of my car. It was all about the maximum thrill I could extract for myself—the adrenaline rush felt so good and clear. If I was out of my fucking mind, I didn't know it.

I gained a reputation as a gear-head. One time, I took the engine out of my car, set it at the end of my driveway by a ditch, and started washing the engine degreaser off with the garden hose. A bunch of friends drove by and stopped.

"Hey Hoffmann," they yelled. "Blow another engine?"

"Nah," I yelled back. "Just cleaning it. Gonna paint it orange."

After a few years, I ended up in court more than once for racing on Gratiot Avenue. I finally decided to sell the Chevelle and buy a little economy car.

Eventually I landed a steady job at an engineering office like my dad's, designing massive machines for the auto industry. With the new cash flow, I started buying sound equipment and helping bands run live shows.

One night, I went home with a girl I met at a bar. We had to sneak in through her parents' backdoor and tiptoe up the stairs to her room so we didn't wake her former coalminer dad. I asked her about the big sliding deadbolt lock on her bedroom door. It stood out because of how crooked it was. She said she locks it at night in case he comes home drunk.

When I woke up, I wiped my palm across her frost covered bedroom window to see a big sprawling industrial complex. I asked her about it. She said it was a bomb factory during the war. The same guy her parents rented their house from owned it. She gave me his name. I was looking for a storage unit for my sound system.

On the way out to my car, I smiled at her mom as I cut through the kitchen, then shuffled through the ankle-deep snow over to a little office building.

I asked the landlord if he had any space. He said he had just the place for me, and showed me a big empty silo of a building. I immediately saw its potential to be my next big creative expression.

Since it didn't have heat, I waited until spring to move in. Right away I built a little sleeping loft, and every day before work I would wake up, take my towel and soap down to the river and strip naked to bathe. There was a ceremonial quality to the ritual. During the spring, it was too cold to step all the way in the river, so I'd lay a small piece of wood at the edge of the water to kneel on, and splash myself with the frigid water.

Over the next five years I gutted that place and built a playhouse of a recording studio inside. I was like a beaver on meth—I kept investing time, kept making it more and more outrageous. I painted the walls bright yellow, installed a massive red curtain I'd found in an abandoned Detroit theatre, mounted an eight-foot-long stuffed marlin trophy on one wall, some mannequin legs with fish-net tights and striped pumps above the door, and situated an old phone booth in a corner.

It wasn't long before bands started coming over to practice. Then some artist friends of mine rented space in the complex as well. They even brought a grand piano. To my joy, a vibrant little artist colony was forming. We called it Boyle-Ville after the owner of the property.

One of the artists was a scenery shop carpenter at a local college's live theatre. Every month or so, the crew would strike a set from a big show and throw it all in their dumpster. We'd go over with a fleet of pickup trucks and haul the set back to the studio, then rebuild it into a wild bastardization of a structure.

Then we'd throw a huge party.

We built an amazing Roman Colosseum dance floor once: multi-level stage, fake marble pillars, plastic foliage arbors and white drapes. The parties grew more outrageous. Soon we added entertainment for when our house bands took set breaks. The one that sticks out was TV toss—we'd play Sousa Marches like the *1812 Overture*, and whenever the cannons fired, we'd throw a TV off the third-story roof and watch it explode onto the concrete pad below.

It was around this time that I joined one of the bands as its bass player, when their existing bass player just stopped coming around. It wasn't that hard. I was at least five years older than the rest of them—they helped me really let go of my rigid engineer self-image. Actually, it was more like they rubbed my face in it—they'd get me to dye my hair red, or dress in edgier outfits for shows. Within a year, we were opening up for some decent headliners in and around Detroit's late '80s punk scene.

The ability to feed my ego was now at new levels. I'd walk on stage riding a euphoric wave, wearing black tights with a "McDonalds Hamburger" T-shirt. Fan girls would rush up just to touch me. I felt so powerful. I'd stretch the mic out over the writhing mosh pit, fans climbing all over themselves, and we'd shout some crazy chorus in unison, "Stink like fish you make me mad, stink like fish you make me sad."

I started dating a hip, creative woman who had just returned from New York City. She was burned out from being a production assistant in the porn industry—she took one look at what I was doing and told me I needed to get out of Detroit, and find something different.

I felt the urgency. Soon I turned my efforts to selling my used Jaguar and sound gear to pay off a ton of loans. I was in New York in less than six months. This was late 1986—all I had to my name was twelve-hundred dollars. Onto another four-year expansion: working at recording studios, creating an award winning short film soundtrack, building sets for Broadway shows, even doing runway lighting for some of the biggest names in fashion.

In a blink of an eye, 20 more years came and went. One day, that same thrust toward life rushed back when I contemplated building the RYNO bike. I knew the feeling. I *missed* the feeling—that visceral embodiment of being so cool that I could ride up to any group of strangers and know they would be curious about who I was and what I was all about.

That *invincible* feeling has a lot of value in our culture. It's at the core of just about any product that promises to help a man display his prowess and achieve his power. I swear: all a dude really wants once in a while is for someone to stop and say, "Oh my god, you are so fucking awesome, attractive *and* sexy for owning that car or boat or one-wheel motorcycle." But since this never really happens, we compensate for the feeling of not being good enough, which really means unworthy of connection.

For me to get my fix, I kept doing more and more showman-type expressions, as if I was becoming addicted *and* resistant to the same drug. I needed a more potent strain to stay regulated, maybe even feel the high again.

○

As a longtime engineer, I know we fall into one of two categories. First, there are those of us who know how to design and build in order to earn our keep, but are humble, and tend to hide our desire to be celebrated. Then there are those who build something, and put neon all over it, fire up a few spotlights, and hire models to stand next to it and hand out brochures.

I emerged from the latter category. But the bigger point is this: no engineer in either category will ever find his primal survival solely dependent on *understanding* other engineers. In fact, being a typical engineer almost requires a certain *ignorance* of ourselves and of others.

We believe in hard work. We believe in an orderly world. We believe we are providing the best that anyone can offer. And we also believe that others can fuck off and bend to our perfect social model because it's so goddamn elegant.

Even with all that stoic work ethic, I believe that many engineers think we're granted a certain privilege. It's hard to argue with the value of a well-oiled machine that sits on a factory floor and coins out parts that can be turned into money.

But what about the people that live with engineers, constantly trying to get through to us? They adapt their behavior so as not to distance or anger us. They try to not be too boisterous, to not complain too much—afraid to bite the hand that feeds them. While they're trying to adapt and shift around us, a lot of engineers high-five each other to reassure ourselves we have it all figured out. After all, we yield results, and our aesthetics are the benchmark for all design.

There are people trying to reach us, but they can't penetrate into our hearts—not because we aren't listening to *them*, but because we aren't listening to *ourselves*.

A man's desire to be invincible, and his particular thrust toward life, can come in many forms. Even violence is a thrust toward life. Too often in our culture, we don't see violence until it's too late, or after it escalates into specific actions. But what about the casual and *accepted* underpinnings of aggression that exist at the roots?

I used to see a woman walking, and if I thought she was HOT, I'd reinforce my own thinking by looking at other dudes and nodding in unison as she walked by. Nothing violent about that, right?

There's a dynamic in play when men say a woman is hot, then take it to the next step by saying she *made him* feel sexy. We're giving up ownership of our erotic feelings; we're putting the pressure solely on the objectified woman. It's totally different than a man saying "I *feel* sexy inside when that woman walks by."

On the other side of the equation, a man who fails to own his sexuality and erotic response will also blame a woman for not being *hot enough* to excite him. It's *her fault* he's not turned on.

And what about when a man says a woman is SO HOT, he simply couldn't *help himself?* This is the very foundation of rape culture.

Until we take a stand and begin owning our erotic expressions, and express pride in being fully expressed individuals, then people of all gender types are going to continue to suffer and struggle to enact their own erotic liberation.

The Marketplace in Nature

Even today, I still wonder about not being good enough, and the drive to overachieve to make up for it. Why was I afraid to just ask for what I wanted? Why didn't I believe I was worthy of getting it? What made it so important to be seen and validated?

I have always been looking for some unifying thesis that could tie it all together and help me make sense of things—to see it in a light that wasn't so over-the-top and ego-driven. Then I stumbled on the bowerbird.

A relatively ugly little bird from Australia and New Guinea, bowerbirds are known for their extraordinarily complex courtship and mating behaviors. Defined as any of a family of passerine birds (*Ptilonorhynchidae*), a male bowerbird builds a highly aesthetic, nest-like structure on the ground—a bower—to attract mates. The bowers look like chambers, complete with arches made of twigs and grasses, and often adorned with brightly colored flower petals and found objects. Whereas a peacock has to work with its feathers, the bowerbird constructs a sophisticated work of art that doubles as an attractive bachelor pad—quite the engineer!

During the courtship season, the male bowerbird continually refines his presentation to attract a mate. There's research that shows how younger males are lucky to be successful even once during the mating season, while older males are killing it! How do they learn to do that, without a word, or song, or neon glow? How do they refine their engineering and design skills to create a more erotically charged display?

The bowerbird example reinforces my primal desire, as a builder, to create from a place that, first off, addresses my need to be seen, and secondly, comes from a thrust of erotically charged passion.

The most fascinating thing to me is this: by building something that attracts attention, the male bowerbird fulfills the most primal urge in all of nature—to pass on its genes. His act is not one of conformity or homogenization, but literally an act rebellion against other male birds.

Often, when we think of courtship among birds, our minds go to music: the song bird in a fruit tree is akin to a flute player below a castle balcony, or a rock guitarist ripping a solo on stage.

Among bowerbirds, something else is going on—a blend of shelter, security, and sexuality, all rolled into one kickass, physical creation. As any engineer can appreciate, the bower is physically THERE, not just a big idea, or a song that comes and goes.

And of course, this is not just a "bird thing." Nor is it solely a "male thing." There are many examples in nature of females creating tremendous expressions of beauty and function to attract a mate. In fact, I believe this drive has nothing to do with gender. We all feel and express it in different ways. This force is at the root of the term *peacocking*. Anyone that wants to show off and be sexy can do it.

In choosing the male bowerbird, I wanted to highlight a builder that's become something of a totem animal for me. Through the bowerbird, I find a meaningful connection to my own drive toward innovation, my relationship to embodied feelings, and my impulse to be erotically awake.

I believe these erotically driven acts are at the heart of our insatiable drive for innovative, technological advances.

How could an engineer design a car as gorgeous and sexy as the Jaguar XK-E? Just looking at it gives me an erotic charge. It's a rolling example of an exquisite expression of art, and a fine rendering of inspired engineering that, at the time, pushed the envelope of performance and handling.

It's one thing to add independent suspension and disc brakes three years before anyone else. But how did Malcolm Sayer, the car's designer, make it look so damn sexy? He was a notable aircraft designer, which in itself requires a skillful interaction with airflow and nature. Still, how did he capture an erotic charge in the lines of the flowing sheet-metal body? Did he work from a felt sense, or a sensory embodiment of dynamic action? Did he know how he wanted the car to "feel," and then attempt to recreate that felt sense during the design? Maybe it came later, as he stepped back and looked at the final clay model, walking back and forth to push the clay around until it felt right. We'll never know.

Does the male bowerbird feel what it wants to display, and then construct its visual ornamentation and patterns in alignment with its feeling? Is it coded in the bird's DNA? Or is the bowerbird a learned apprentice, having watched and studied other bowerbirds for hundreds of hours? If so, then how many thousands of years has that tradition been handed down?

There's so much we don't understand about the interplay between an erotic mating drive and a practical, creative innovator. That's why it's so important to find the curiosity to step out of what feels normal and familiar, thrust ourselves into the unknown, and get lost once in a while.

We don't create out of emptiness, but out of chaos.

When we discover erotic play, the idea of being lost becomes an altered state of mind that connects our creative drive to a form of magic. In an altered, trance-like consciousness, three hours can go by without us knowing. Think back to your youth: how often did you get lost in your thoughts, or a book, or a game in the woods with friends? Someone, an adult, would call us back to the real world—dinner was ready, or it was bath time, or we needed to get our homework done.

Today, in this lost state we can communicate non-verbally through the language of the body. Like a dance, the body knows where to go—we just need to *let go* of needing to get anything from the experience. When we loosen our grip, let things roll, and follow a moment's essence, we enter into the realm from where our most potent and creative acts of inspiration exist. Once there, we can bring them forth. Later, once we "come back to reality," we can use the discerning intellectual mind to apply design constraints, and push things toward profound innovations.

Building my Alter Ego

Toward the end of my marriage, Jean must have been confused when I decided to build a Satyr costume—part goat, part lascivious human. I went full-bore, from the flowers and horns on my head, to the tail, right down to cloven hooved boots.

I had a steady engineering job, the house renovation was all but done, and I had pretty much given up on the idea of she and I having a deep, satisfying, erotic relationship. I'd been hiding my frustration, and needed to prove to myself I could do something to satisfy my need to enact a purely visceral thrill of rebellion.

One day, a costume party showed up on one of my community lists. There was a competition, too. Having pumped so much physical energy into restoring the house, my body was in top physical condition.

This would be the perfect opportunity to capture and put my alter ego on grand display. The Satyr would be my personal "fuck you" to everything that seemed to blocking me from making contact with my deeper, wilder nature.

For my head, I fashioned a wreath of vines and leaves, and attached a pair of small horns. I made sideburns from the same fake fur that covered the front of my G-string. On the back I secured an upturned, eight-inch tail, stuffed tightly for a nice fat look—it sat at the top of my ass crack so convincingly, it could have been real. Looking at it in the mirror, a wave came over me, like I was reconnecting with some lost aspect of myself—a truly arcane feeling. It allowed me to feel the mythic beast inside myself, through which I could channel and turn my frustration into beauty.

When I started building the boots, I fully understood what my subconscious was up to: I wanted to access something from another world, have it run through my entire body and self, and take on the poise of its stance.

I had a sense of how I wanted to feel as I moved in those boots—statuesque and strutting gracefully. My engineer brain went to work to figure out how to make a pair of calf-high, furry boots with elevated ankles that looked like an animal's hooves. I started with some wood blocks for the four-inch tall platforms, cut the cloven hoof shape, sanded them, and painted them black. I screwed down a pair of running shoes at the front, which allowed the heel of the shoe to lift off the wooden base, giving me the graceful freedom I wanted. Then I wrapped everything in fake brown fur, and added long, wispy strands around the back to hide the tall heel.

This was no mere "cosplay" costume. It captured a deeply mythic Beltane-like pagan antiquity. The moment came to stand in our living room, my transformation complete. Jean didn't know what to do with herself. She looked at me from a few feet away—hesitant, curious—but couldn't engage with me.

At the party, my experience was completely different. Woman after woman approached and asked to have their "dance with the Satyr Man" experience. I was on fire all night, dancing into the mystery of what I had called forth to enact.

Building and dressing up as the Satyr rekindled the same fear and exhilaration I experienced as a kid, when I'd run out in the front yard naked for a second, then run right back inside. I wanted to test my fear of being seen, with a hidden hope that someone would accept and love me in my nakedness.

Somehow, I was more "me" as the Satyr than I ever was in the "engineer-husband" costume I wore for two decades.

I had innovated from the gut and soul, used my heart and mind to create new skin, and found the courage to step into it.

The Mattress

Three days after I walked out my own front door, my mother called me.

"I just got off the phone with your *wife*," she pointedly began. "It sounds like everyone is losing their minds. You need to get your butt over there and instill some order. You're a Hoffmann, for God's sake. You need to *fix this*."

There was the magic word—FIX. It was just like my mom to show no real interest in what I was experiencing, or what was actually happening for me. She had no curiosity about how I was, or what my plan looked like. And she had zero interest in listening to me. To her, the job was simple: fix it.

A therapist friend helped me figure out how best to handle the situation. She suggested that any time I went back to the house, I should knock, rather than just walk in the front door. This would send a clear message to Jean that I had left, that I'm committed to creating a firm boundary, and that the house was a safe place for her.

I called Jean to let her know I was coming over. Once I arrived, I parked in the driveway and took a deep breath. Stepping up onto the porch, I realized this was the beginning I could have never imagined when I left the house a few days ago. I was so focused on getting out, I never considered what happened next. Now, standing here for the first time since leaving, I was determined to retain respect for Jean and everything we had built together. I did not want to make the split anyone's fault, or look for a reason to destroy something as a way to gain the courage I needed make my own choices.

Right away, Jean started into a barrage of questions, most of which cycled through fear. What were we going to do? Why was this happening? What about the house? There wasn't much anger, but she was definitely dead set on the idea that the world was coming to an end. All I could offer was that things would be all right. I even shared something that sounded like a plan, complete with a timeline.

I left Jean in the kitchen and walked into Lauren's room. I wanted to see how she was, and to try my best and at least reassure her things would be fine.

"How come your plan is so different than Mommy's?" she asked. "I don't know who to believe." Her words hit me hard. This was going to be a long haul—I needed to pace myself.

I went back to the kitchen and asked Jean if there was anything in the house that needed my attention. This was our love language, one of the consistent threads through our 20-year marriage. She immediately started making a list.

☼

The upheaval settled into a rhythm that continued for six months. I'd go to the house and take care of all the last minute renovations—we were going to put it on the market. Sometimes Jean was there, sometimes not. When we talked, we kept it basic, did our best not to trigger one another. Though our marriage had lacked passion, we'd always respected each other.

One day when Lauren was around, I casually mentioned to her that I needed a mattress, but didn't say much else. Then I headed back to my rented room, which held a folding chair, a little TV table where I kept my laptop, an air mattress, and a carry-on piece of luggage with my clothes.

Two hours later, Jean called from IKEA—there was a mattress in the return section marked half-off. The very woman who cursed me as I walked out the door was now guarding a mattress for me.

I drove to IKEA and saw Jean in the returns area. I was confused about how to engage with her, and decided to just walk up casually, focusing on our friendship rather than our fractured marriage.

I followed her to the mattress. We walked through the checkout line together—she even helped me load the mattress onto the rolling cart, and hung around as I muscled it atop the roof of my car and tied it down.

We exchanged a few words—casual things, friendly things, but nothing about what was clearly the elephant in the parking lot. I waved goodbye and drove off in a daze.

Marriages go through tough times, I heard myself thinking. *Maybe this was just another one. Maybe I'm being stupid. Maybe we can fix this.* It was that same familiar feeling of being responsible for someone else's pain and suffering. I hated that feeling, and the second guessing that came with such a gut-wrenching decision. I was at the threshold of creating something new, of claiming my choice and knowing it was good.

The road back to my room passed by an old shortcut that went straight to our house. I'd made that turn so many times it was baked into my muscle memory. I felt the car begin to veer in that direction—my mind went into overdrive.

"How stupid am I?" I asked myself out loud. "All I have to do is go back to the house and rescue this. Things will be okay."

I was at the turn. I had the green light. We needed a new mattress for the guest room anyway.

Then something deep inside my chest reached up and steadied the wheel—like an arm from another lifetime coming in and taking over. The wheel stayed straight. I kept going—sailed right through the intersection and toward my new horizon.

PART 3:
LETTING GO

Once I started to understand the relationship between eroticism and design, I realized the RYNO bike was my own personal bower. My engineering brain knew how to add features to a product, but it wasn't until I started waking up my erotic awareness that I understood how to design "sexy." Knowing how to present an erotic display—while being conscious of its inherent vulnerability—allowed me to create a RYNO design that resonated as a powerful tool to attract attention.

It Needs to Scale

After a year of finishing all the little renovations to get the house on the market, clearing out my personal belongings, and helping Jean and Lauren move into a new place, the money from closing finally landed in my checking account.

It was a rare time in my life to lie in bed in my little rented room and feel peace of mind. I let days go by riding my mountain bike, soaking in the hot tub behind the house, and lounging in the hot sun naked.

Something else was going on at this time—the second RYNO prototype, the same one I'd crashed, was back on the road. It had taken half a year to rebuild and rewire it. By now, I was riding it around downtown Portland—testing it for my own understanding, and also discovering what the bike meant to people.

It was amazingly versatile. I could take it onto a light rail train car, or into an elevator with six people, and no one seemed bothered or troubled. In fact, the bike fascinated people. Strangers would stop me at every turn to ask about it, touch it, have their picture taken with it. For me, the attention was validation, a reminder to keep going.

When I wasn't riding, or lounging, I was busy designing RYNO's next version. To fit within street-legal regulations, it needed to have a top speed of no more than 25 miles per hour, and a maximum electric motor power of 700 watts.

I started making full-size sketches with fat Sharpie pens. I'd lay the prints out on my bed, stare, then allow myself to feel the struggle as I tried to arrive at something I was proud of. This obsessive design phase went on for months. To counter it, I'd get back on the bike and cruise, or lie on my bed and look up at the Christmas lights twinkling in the tree branches I'd installed like a canopy overhead. I would walk, meditate, and dance. Any time my brain felt squeezed, I'd come back to my body. And that voice would kick up again—*you gotta feel your way, Chris.*

After spending the entire summer designing the new RYNO, I finally built all the parts for a prototype. I hired a friend to shoot some photos, and before the control system was even done, we launched a website to announce that RYNO was here. A shiny, new, street-legal, single wheel motorcycle at an outrageous price tag—$25,000.

Then something unexpected happened: five orders came in. And not just local or regional—the RYNO buzz had gone global, and the orders were from all around the world.

I was completely intoxicated by the idea of success. I spent most of the money I got from the house sale on all the parts I'd need. Then I started building. Forget that the software was still in development, or that we hadn't even begun testing the new lower-powered 700 watt motors. I was in the thick of it—drunk on the feeling of eminent success, and following the energy. Things were moving, and there was no time to rest.

✲

A prominent local lawyer who happened to be a good friend introduced me to Tony, a newly retired start-up veteran looking for a project he could get behind—one that wouldn't cause him too much stress. He came over to my shop. I was bouncing off the walls with excitement, manically going on and on about how huge it was all going to be.

That's when Tony stopped me cold.

"Listen," he started, "if you build those five bikes, you're going to end up stuck in this garage the rest of your life."

I heard him right away. From the way he said it, to the clarity in his body language, to the tone of voice—it was like he pressed his big thumb down on my pause button.

"Let's sit down and write a business plan," he continued. "If we can't prove this thing will scale, then you're wasting your time."

Instinctively, I knew Tony was right. I needed to bring some logic back into the equation. That doesn't mean it was easy for me to let go of the spell I was under—or to admit to him that I agreed. Speed, energy, urgency, money—they make for an intoxicating brew.

This was a critical moment, both from a business standpoint, and also my own stamina. I knew myself well enough. Once I had a clear plan, I'd switch to implementation. From there, I'd harness up and pull the load until I was exhausted.

It took me a few days to come to grips with his challenge, get out of my ego, and start thinking strategically again. Then I finally got the nerve to call and tell him he was right.

It wasn't as simple as just sitting down and writing a plan. At Tony's insistence, I returned the $15,000 in deposits I'd received for the bikes. I then scrapped or returned all of the parts I'd bought, keeping only enough for one bike. Instead of spending the next half-year building, framing, and forging forward in that direction, I turned my attention to gathering real market data, which sounded about as sexy as clipping my toenails.

Every time it got tough, or boring, or existentially depressing—times when I just wanted to say fuck it and make up the numbers—Tony would counter with logic and reason.

"I'm not going to sit in an investor meeting," he'd start, "and when they ask about the numbers, say, 'Oh, we just made them up.' They'll smell bullshit a mile away."

Tony knew the big truth: investors can't possibly verify how smart you say you are, and they know it. They want to see a plan so they can see how you're going to *reduce the risk* for follow-on investors. That's where Tony sold them on the fact that we would test the market so we could get smarter.

This was familiar ground for Tony. He'd spent decades negotiating multi-million dollar international contracts, and had sat in on hundreds of investment meetings. He had my complete trust.

It wasn't long before Tony became RYNO's first COO. He saved the company's ass day after day—and my ass as well. What he brought to the table never changed: strategic insight, a demand for transparency, and unwavering integrity.

※

When we finally completed the software development for the new street-legal prototype, it failed miserably. The motor wasn't powerful enough, and the control system refused to balance. It was almost impossible to steer, and definitely not safe enough to ride.

Had I built those five bikes, instead of just the one prototype, I would have spent the whole next year scrambling to salvage what I'd built, managing irate customers, and trying to figure out how to return the deposit money I would have no doubt spent—and then some.

Thanks to Tony's experience of knowing what NOT to do, we created more time for ourselves doing what *we had to do* to make things right. More importantly, something bigger was about to find RYNO. I didn't know what it was yet—but I could feel it.

Learning to Lead

Back in my early machine design days in Detroit, there was always a healthy level of competition between the engineering department and the machine-shop floor. At my first engineering job at a Portland machine building company, the competition was so fierce it was almost combative. Even so, I made it a priority to build a strong relationship with the machine-shop foreman. Regardless of the tension, we actually enjoyed each other.

This foreman was an interesting dude, kind of young for the role, but lots of street smarts. He'd been an iron worker and was almost killed when a 200-pound bundle of re-bar fell off a crane hook and went sailing past his shoulder while he was suspended 100 feet up. The machine shop workers loved him. He and I shared lots of closed-door meetings where we laughed and shook our heads at the high school level of drama among grown men.

It was mid-week when the owner of the company stopped by my office to ask me if I could fit in a job on a tight timeline. He said it was important to him to open a relationship with Boeing, and this was a job that no other company would touch. It had to be done in 10 days, and installed on a Saturday because it was a holiday, the only day Boeing's production line would be shut down for months.

We needed to design a loader that could transfer a 5,000-pound steel pallet that held 20-foot-long aircraft parts from a load position into a high temperature cleaning oven. There was one design constraint: in order to open the oven door, the loader had to retract 12 feet, and then extend to bridge the gap without sagging more than half an inch. More than that, the track rollers would not engage with the track rails inside the oven. I agreed to take the job because I knew my best lead engineer was just coming off of a project.

We went at it hard with a clear focus on designing something we could fabricate in our shop using as many off-the-shelf, local parts as possible. After a few days, my engineer had a solid design coming together. With my years of experience designing highly complex automation and machinery, I could tell it wasn't going to be structurally sound enough to pass the test. I mentioned my concerns to him in an offhand kind of way—I wanted to get a sense of his confidence. He said he wasn't worried, but would do the math to double check.

The next morning, I checked back with him. He confirmed the calculations were right on. I still wasn't convinced. In looking closer at the drawing, I could see an open area through the middle of the support frame where we could add a few pieces of square tubing to increase its beam strength. I made it a point to wander down to talk to my shop foreman buddy and explained what was happening. The load test needed to go down first thing Friday morning if we were going to have time to recover from a possible failure and still install the machine on Saturday. I asked my foreman buddy if he had a few 20-foot lengths of 4X4 inch steel tubing on the welding rack. He wasn't sure, but understood my thinking. He said he'd make sure to have a few lengths by Friday.

On Monday, I released all the drawings to the shop exactly the way my engineer designed the structure. After a week of 12-hour days welding, assembly, and wiring the control system, the shop triumphantly had the machine ready to load test on Friday morning.

At 8 a.m., there was quite a gathering of people, some of whom I didn't even recognize. It's amazing how the chance of failure draws a crowd. I even saw the owner of the company walk onto the balcony that looked out over the expansive shop.

At 30-feet long, the new machine sat in the middle of the largest bay. The guys were loading wooden pallets with everything they could find in the shop to hit the 5,000-pound test weight. As the forklift driver placed the final loaded pallet on the transfer slide, my lead engineer hit the cycle-start button to extend the loader out to the test mark.

With a robotic whine, the motor engaged and sent the slide slowly extending 12 feet out into open air. As it approached the test cone, it was clearly sagging. It slowed to a stop, hit the cone, and knocked it right over. The shop went WILD. A roar came up from the crowd like a crash at the Indy 500.

To add to the humiliation, one shop guy walked up and jumped on the end of the sagging transfer slide, bouncing on it like a diving board. I looked over at the shop foreman, who pantomimed a raised eyebrow and whistling puckered lips—a classic, "that didn't go so well" expression. I glanced over at my engineer, who was standing frozen and clueless.

I cupped my hands around my mouth.

"We need 20 minutes!"

My engineer and I walked upstairs to the engineering office. We stood staring at his CAD model. I asked what he wanted to do. He looked at the drawings carefully.

"Man, if I had a few 20-foot-long pieces of 4X4, I could double up the transfer beam and it would be fine. But I doubt we have that."

"Let's go look." I said.

We went down to the steel rack and poked around. He had his tape measure and was amazed to see two of them right on top. In under 20 minutes, I had him fix the drawing and run it down to the shop. The beams were welded in, and we were ready for a repeat load test right after lunch.

With the same crowd looking on, my engineer hit the start button again. The slide was now so stiff, it cleared the marker cone with a quarter inch to spare. In classic working dude style, everyone in the shop just turned and shuffled away—no applause, no comradery. My engineer went alone up the far steps to the office. I intentionally walked right past my shop foreman buddy. I turned my head slowly to face him, imitating the same puckered lip expression he flashed a few hours ago. In response, he just gave a long low nod of respect. That's all we ever said about it.

There are a lot of different ways that situation could have gone down. I could have gone on a power trip and made an example of my engineer in front of everyone. Or, I could have micro-managed the situation early, and forced him to add the beams at the start. But what would he have learned other than how to take orders?

Power at the expense of others is a mask for insecurity, and a lack of self-confidence and self-worth. If a manager needs to redirect attention toward him or herself, other people will disengage with owning their own creative process. They'll know they're not serving their own expression, but are instead giving it up to feed their boss's ego.

Finding My Inner Rhythm

Before I left my marriage, I went to a three-day music festival in rural Oregon. I had no idea what to expect. It was set at a rolling 20-acre farm with a swimming pond and a shady forested camping ground. I pitched my tent, met my neighbors, and soon found myself sitting on a grassy rise in front of an open pavilion where a band was setting up.

As some pre-show music played, a man and a woman walked onto the empty stage and started dancing. I couldn't figure out what they were doing. It wasn't dancing like I'd seen before. It was more like a highly choreographed performance done by an ordinary couple in their 30s.

They would run at each other and somehow, knowing how to catch one another, they would swing around and land perfectly. He lifted her gracefully and pitched her through the air. They dramatically pushed and pulled at one other. At one point, he bent her head back by her hair, and held her there while they kissed. Then he swung her around, and she ran off to circle back as if they were pretending to be fighting in a gladiator ring.

It went on this way for at least half an hour. The sexual energy and passion between them was palpable. I imagined when they were done dancing, they would have to go off somewhere and have wild primal sex together. It was such a visceral inspiration for me—I knew in that moment I wanted to learn how to dance like that.

Since I lived in Portland, it wasn't long before I discovered the form was called Ecstatic Dance. At its core, Ecstatic Dance was free-form—there was no structure to it. There was a DJ, a sound system, and a room full of people dancing in whatever way they felt like. Some groups practiced facilitated movements, while others felt more like low-impact physical improvisations.

I found an Ecstatic Dance gathering that met weekly in a studio above a bar in North Portland. Every Sunday morning, a couple hundred people gathered. Everyone entered the space in their own states of mind. Regardless of the baggage, stories, or needs they carried in with them, they were there to share the love of dance.

My first few times, I mainly sat along the wall and tried to figure out what the hell I was looking at. It was like an exotic drink made with one-part karate competition, two-parts break-dancing, with a yoga class cherry floating on top. I took an immediate liking to what was unfolding around me.

There was no discernable technique or style. A few couples danced together, drifted in and out of each other's space, then moved on and danced with someone else. How did that happen? What signaled them to do one thing or the other?

Most of the people were lost in their own inner worlds of movement. If lying on the floor and kicking your feet was your dance, then THAT WAS YOUR DANCE. No explanation needed.

At my third weekly dance, just as I was ready to begin exploring my own interactions in this safe, non-judgmental environment, a woman came by and extended her hand for me to join. I stood up and followed her to the middle of the dance floor. She held both of her hands out. I met her invitation, and we began to move in unison. She painted wide sweeping patterns with her arms as I managed to keep a light touch on her palms.

"Push," she whispered. I leaned in and gave her some of my weight. She started moving around me in a squat, like a wrestler looking for an opening. I could feel her strength as we shifted on our feet. She looked me right in the eyes the entire time. Silently, her body energetically spoke to me.

"Push me. Who are you anyway? What does your body want to tell me? Show me."

Then she offered me the lead. I pushed her around playfully, and she responded just enough to show that she was with my every stride.

Our dance was so euphoric and sexy, I could barely take it in. I slowed it way down as we pivoted around in a big circle, our foreheads pressed together. At the end of the song, she stood up, held her hands to her lips in a gentle silent prayer, and walked off. I drifted off to the side and sat down.

What the hell was that?

I soon became a regular. I developed the ability to initiate a dance with women and men. It took great courage for me to drift slowly by a woman, see if her eyes met mine, and discern if she was open to a dance. Could I linger at a distance without crowding her space? Could I wait until she saw me, then offer an invitation? Could I extend an open hand, knowing that she might say "no thanks"?

Engaging with men was different. All it took was to lean against a dude and offer your weight. It would usually move into a *mano-a-mano* exercise in strength exchange, but once in a while, one of us would offer a certain surrender for the other to hold.

I practiced one dance engagement attempt after another. I improvised over and over during the course of a year before I felt like I had an understanding of this practice. Eventually I cultivated a handful of dance partners. I became more courageous, did a few lifts, and slowly became in tune with how my body wanted to move.

Like wearing costumes, dance allows us to express ourselves; at the same time, it reveals our state of being. Movement is a clear transmission of your authentic self. It's hard to hide your inner landscape when you're dancing. That's what makes it such a profound practice—we have no choice but to allow ourselves to just BE.

I discovered that some women love to dance in an erotic container, like they're dancing naked in front of a mirror in their own bedroom. They come to dance to experience and communicate a very private form of sensuality in a safe, public forum. It's unfortunate that women, and men for that matter, don't have more safe places to do this in their lives.

Initially, like many men, I struggled with not taking women's open sensual expression as an implicit invitation. With a sense of deep respect for what I was witnessing, I allowed myself to feel the thrill and beauty of it. As time went on, I became more accustomed to being around that level of beauty, and not attaching any meaning to it.

Honesty is All We Have

A year after I met Tony, RYNO's first COO—a full three years into self-funding RYNO with my own side money—I finally attracted the attention of an angel investor fund. RYNO Motors made it all the way through the vetting funnel, and landed in deep due-diligence.

The investor fund's team of 12 former high-tech company founders and executives ran RYNO through a battery of questions—they needed to find any holes that would take us out of the running. Every time they asked us a question, Tony or I would answer it with a 12-page report, a pie chart, and a spread sheet.

These meetings were grueling and exhausting, but they made us smarter. Tony, who by then had climbed every major mountain peak on the West Coast and a few in Europe, had been a pro squash player, was a seasoned start-up founder, and an alumni of Intel, approached the whole thing with a certain competitive satisfaction. I, however, was intimidated by the whole affair.

They were seasoned business professionals talking a language I so much wanted to emulate. I left high school in a rebellious fit, landed an engineering job, and never made it close to college. Most of my writing skills were developed from creating proposals for engineering projects. I wondered often what they really thought of me. Did I need to be cut from the same cloth as them? Did I sound professional enough? Did I seem like I knew what I was getting into? Did they trust me enough to invest their money in me?

After getting ground in due-diligence for almost six months, it all came down to a demo in the parking garage below their offices. I knew this was my final shot before they were going to put my company to a vote in front of the entire 65-member voting body.

I wore my best suit, prepared myself with lots of facts and figures, and carried an attitude that I was sure they would recognize as professional and put together. I parked my jeep in the parking structure and went around to drag the bike out of the back. There was always a moment where the same recurring thoughts came back again. How many more times would I have to haul the RYNO beast out of yet another car trunk before I could hire someone to do it? How long would I be building prototypes? Maybe I'd *always* be building prototypes until the day I die.

I turned on the bike's power key, stood next to it, and looked down toward the entrance to the elevators where we agreed to meet. I was as ready as I could ever be.

I swung my leg over the bike, and noticed in that instant that the feeling of what the RYNO really meant to me had returned. I genuinely wanted it to be a success—not just for me, but for the sheer joy it brought to others. I didn't care about making a ton of money. I mean, sure, I wanted to do well—why else was I risking my whole career on it? But fame and fortune were not my main drivers. To make it worth it for me, it had to be on my own terms.

I wasn't the type of *professional guy* the investors were. I didn't know how to be one of them. But I did know that I accepted them for who they were. Within that awareness, I trusted that they accepted me as a true innovator.

My whole body relaxed. I wasn't worried about promoting myself, or sharing the list of facts and figures in my head. I switched gears into being a calm-yet-passionate inventor. They immediately responded to my authentic enthusiasm for what I was doing.

One by one, they lined up to ride the bike. I ran next to each of them and shared how excited I was about my invention as they rode it around. The energy was fun and engaging. They all had a great experience, and thanks to my software engineer, the bike performed perfectly.

Two days later, RYNO went up for a vote. We won $1.2 million dollars.

Call in the Project Manager

With all the sudden pressure and focus on the company, I longed for some form of relationship stability again. A year out of my marriage, I knew I wasn't skillful enough to survive in the dating world, nor was I quite ready yet to bear the pain of being alone. After the stuck feeling of my marriage, I wanted something that was dynamic and fun. When I met a vibrant woman named Annie at a friend's house, we practically dropped into an "instant relationship."

With Annie, it was like throwing gasoline on a fire—daring, impulsive, hot. Our bodies felt familiar to each other. My entire physicality lit up when I was with her.

We were on the same page with our relationship. We both wanted something that was super-sexy and long-term. Plus, she was interested in getting to know my daughter better, who was almost 18 at the time. I thought I'd finally figured it all out.

There were some hints along the way that we were hiding aspects of ourselves from each other. I could see the shadows start to form, but I was so swept up in the blend of new passion and familiarity that I ignored them.

Sure enough, before long, I literally started repeating the same relationship dynamic as my marriage.

One day we were making love on the couch, because it felt daring to do so in the middle of the afternoon when people were around just outside. The next day, I would find myself trying to fix her broken emotions, worried about her feelings to the point where I was—once again—dismissing my own.

A few months in, our "perfect relationship" began to unravel into ugly bouts of confrontation. In our first few fights, I found myself apologizing early on, whether or not I'd actually done something. I just wanted the bad feelings to end so we could get back to the good as soon as possible. Then I started feeling attacked, and sensed that these attacks were disproportionate to the reality of whatever I'd said or done. I tried to focus on what I did to upset her, approaching these moments from genuine curiosity and respect. She kept questioning WHY I was acting certain ways, and doing things she didn't approve of. It felt like a controlling yank on a choker collar.

As the bouts escalated, rather than apologizing, I began taking a more open stance, trying to facilitate a conversation, one where we could both come at things from a place of open understanding. Sometimes it worked. Often it didn't because of how defensive I felt.

Subconsciously, what I was really doing was trying to get her back to a regulated emotional state so I could return to mine—the same thing I would do for my mom and my ex. By being so adaptable and accommodating to *her* needs, I wasn't standing up for myself. After my placid, semi-unconscious marriage, the idea of fighting was foreign to me. It was way easier to just fix what was broken, and not rebuild it. Such a classic engineer's approach. Keep adding bailing wire, duct tape and spackling until the original object is no longer recognizable. I was at a total loss where healthy disagreements, or difficult truths, or outright manipulation started and ended.

Fuck.

I couldn't simply let go of my impulse to control, and give Annie the space she needed to regulate her own experience—or better yet, make it clear she needed to be responsible for her own regulation. I didn't know how to be at peace with myself, and couldn't trust her capacity to reconnect with me when she was ready. Space, time, awareness—these things are foreign to an engineer obsessed with the idea of *making everything right*."

One thing I do know about myself: I've always had an internal project manager I could count on to intervene when I was in an emotional funk. This is the same project manager that would get my ass out of bed on a Monday morning after being laid off for six months, grab the Sunday classifieds, find one job to apply for, and hammer on it until I got it. He's also the manager that would listen to reason. He lives under my porch like a personal bridge troll, always there whether I need him or not.

No matter how bamboozled I felt by any situation, or how emotionally overwhelmed I became, at some point my project manager would speak up and yell, "Listen, that's bullshit. Fuck all that. We've got shit to do."

Annie was not a fan of my project manager.

That should have been a further indicator of bad things to come. My project manager's probing logical questions, tied to actual events and agreements, made it frustratingly impossible for her to keep imposing her reality over mine. There were so many times I should have left our relationship. She was *gaslighting* me before I even knew what that concept was. I drew a line in the sand that she walked right past with an anxious smile. I let her do it over and over because I thought it was easier for me to meet her needs than to experience the anxiety of how hard it was for her. I let her do it because I didn't yet have the courage to push the relationship beyond crisis and into change.

It took three years for me to learn one seemingly obvious lesson: the only person I ever have control over is *myself*. After countless boundary breaches and emotional drama-fests, my project manager was literally screaming bloody murder to begin the process of leaving, no matter how painful.

Obviously, Annie and I were not a good fit—not for the time, and not for what we were looking for in a long-term relationship. I clearly hadn't healed from my marriage. Thanks to Annie, I finally accepted this fact. I needed some new operational tools if I was ever going to open my heart. I was desperate to find a love that was big and meaningful; at the same time, I was frozen in fear at the mere suggestion of trying again.

There was a time in my life when I was afraid of my inner project manager. When I was younger, he never hung around long enough to show his more mature side—he'd explode into a situation, clear-cut his way through the mess, and leave well before anyone knew what had happened. He was just like the time my dad grabbed and threw me against a coat rack, demanding I never fight with my brother again. Problem identified, problem solved. But with Annie, my project manager finally took a seat at the table, and helped me sort through my life. I felt like he was protecting me now—not just from the world, but from myself.

A Test of Faith in Shenzhen

With a slow start, and having taken us a year longer than we thought to finalize the software and get the bike in production, RYNO Motors was about to run out of cash. I watched my emails closely. Since the bike was a media magnet, I received all kinds of random and ridiculous inquiries that where cryptic and sometimes hard to believe. On one particular morning, as I was looking at our dwindling bank balance, I received an email from an Asian investor. Two weeks later, he and I were signing an informal agreement for him to invest.

After completing this first investment, I agreed to fly to Hong Kong and do a demo ride to help him interest more investors. I packed the bike into four boxes, and $1,200 later checked them into the belly of a 747. I got stuck in San Francisco for a night because of fog, then flew 13 hours. A driver picked me up and took me directly to a Ducati motorcycle dealership for the first demo.

In the sticky, late night heat, I bolted the bike together in a back workshop, then loaded the batteries and looked at the blinking balance button. With any new product, and especially just before demo, there's that moment: will this fucking thing light up? I took a breath, pressed the button, and the bike balanced. I rolled the bike out to the showroom floor, and rocked the demo in front of a handful of potential investors.

Thank goodness *that* was behind me. I figured that was enough excitement for one trip. Then, my main investor threw a surprise at me—he and his group wanted to smuggle the bike into China for a demo in Shenzhen the following day.

I had no idea who these guys were except for the main investor, and I'd only known him a few weeks. Before I could even think about it, a Mercedes rolled up. Two dudes jumped out of the front, took the spare tire out of the trunk, and replaced it with the RYNO's entire wheel assembly—imbedded with all of our software and technology. Then they loaded the bike's upper frame into a van that suspiciously appeared at just that moment. I stood there like I was in a James Bond movie, completely overwhelmed by the intrusiveness and bold momentum of it all. There wasn't any time to actually contemplate what was happening, let alone check in with *myself* and decide if I was okay with any of it.

I watched that black sedan thunder off into the narrow warehouse-lined street, humping through the rain-filled potholes. The investor just smiled.

"Don't worry," was all he said. He motioned to a BMW that, naturally, just suddenly appeared. We both got in, and the car raced through the dark alleys of Hong Kong, then hurled out across a massive white suspension bridge with the entire Hong Kong harbor lit up off to the right.

The car parked in front of a small youth hostel in Kowloon. I fell asleep in a room barely big enough for the bed, woke up and wandered around the neighborhood in search of something to eat. Then I headed back to my room and waited for someone to knock on my door. That was literally all I could do—I had no idea where the RYNO was, or how I was eventually going to meet up with it.

When the knock finally came, I grabbed my suit jacket and went with some complete stranger, who drove to the Chinese border. I had to walk through the checkpoint, get my passport stamped, and then wait for someone else to pick me up and take me to a huge nightclub packed with investors.

The RYNO was already there. It stood tall in the middle of a stripper cage, lit up with a mirror ball. Four Asian models posed next to it, RYNO logos on their tight T-shirts, which were tucked into small red booty shorts—their skinny legs stretched down to infinity. *That* image is burnt into my dude brain for good. They strutted languidly around the perimeter of the small dance floor in black stilettos while some dude juggled lit Molotov cocktails to a rocking DJ.

The investor gave me a nod—I didn't know what it meant, so I decided to walk up to the RYNO, maneuver it out of the stripper cage, and ride it around in a circle. The software was barely working—the bike could do something random at any second. I made a few laps, smiled at the girls with each pass, and kept an eye on the cocktail juggler as his show wound down.

There was no plan to any of it—no set-up conversation, no bullet points about what to expect, how to act, what to do. No idea of timing whatsoever. I just saw an opening and figured I'd fill it. As I rode the bike around, the investor walked onto the dance floor with a microphone. I parked and walked up to him as he started an introduction. Nearby, our RYNO teaser video started playing on a jumbo screen.

He introduced the RYNO in Mandarin, then leaned over to me.

"Tell us a story about who you are and how RYNO was built," he whispered. Then he introduced me as the CEO of RYNO Motors. A big round of applause went up.

I was in total disbelief about what this guy had pulled off in such a short amount of time. How did he get all the men and women here? The place was packed—people standing, sitting, waiting. The energy pumped through in an exhausting blur.

When it was over, I rolled the bike out the front door, into a massive, Olympic Village-like plaza, all lit up in twinkling lights. As I waited next to the bike for the rest of the crew, a woman ran up to me.

"Your body has the brightest light I have ever seen in my entire life," she touchingly said.

Soon I was whisked to a massage palace, the size of a hotel on the Vegas strip—the lobby was at least three stories tall. They directed me into a lavish spa area and gave me a locker for my stuff. I changed into a robe and slippers. A crew of us soaked in a shallow, steaming hot pool—huge, about the size of four tennis courts, tiles throughout, and marble columns lining the perimeter. Against the back wall, four glazed dragon heads spouted firehose streams of water from their mouths. I stood there naked, thigh-deep in the pool, and let the water from one of those dragons bathe every inch of my body.

There was so much spectacle to business dealing in China—even restaurant lobbies resembled the Monterey Aquarium, but the fish were there to be eaten. Karaoke was in private rooms where every businessman had a girl on each arm, to ply him with booze and egg him on to sing another. Was this about creating some kind of real connection between the men? Or was it all about competition? There was definitely a vulnerability to it. We went from suits to nakedness, to drinks, to singing, all in a matter of hours. And women were constantly serving us in the most docile ways.

After drying off, the main investor took me to a lounge and pointed at a back-lit display where I was to pick my masseuse for the night. There were about 50 of them like little color photos of hamburgers in a fast food restaurant. I had a flashback to Dave Lee's apartment all those years ago—a row of printed, two-dimensional faces smiling at me. I scanned each one in search of any ounce of empathy, or a sign of a life energy that might be fun to connect with, but they all looked hopelessly the same, a series of blank-faced soap models with porcelain skin.

I wound up choosing one not because of her eyes or lips, but because I liked her number. The madam called for her. When she appeared, head bowed, she led me to my room. The investor mentioned that he booked back-to-back 90-minute sessions—I could spend the whole night right across the hall.

In my room, the woman took my robe from my shoulders, hung it on a little wooden peg, and motioned for me to lie face down on the white sheet. She pulled a sheet up over me and disappeared. The sliding doorway was rice paper covered bamboo. I lay there quietly, but less than a minute later, the madam's voice shot through the entire place—she was yelling at patrons in another room. This went on every 10 minutes or so for the rest of the night.

When my masseuse returned I almost didn't hear her. I rolled my head to the right to see her slip out of her little gown and hang it up as if she'd done it a thousand times. Her pert, bare breasts looked almost too pure for my eyes. I scanned down to see a pair of white lace panties, down farther to see her feet in a pair of grass woven slippers.

The image was so very vulnerable and intimate in the dim light, I almost forgot to breathe. She moved over and knelt down to start my massage.

It was the oddest thing I ever experienced. Nothing like the sensual trance I remembered with Magdalena—more like a cat pawing all over my back with no sense of pressure variation or connection to what she was doing. It went on and on for an hour—no rhythm or change in cadence. It was more agitating than anything. I finally motioned for her to stop.

She was confused, but I conveyed my wish to where she took out a small blue card and pointed at a list of increasing costs. I remember the investor mentioning not to pay more than a 150 RMB. She kept pointing at two hundred, so I paid her that anyway. The second woman came in a half hour later and immediately turned on the TV above the bed. I motioned for her to just leave me alone, and she left.

It was 2 a.m. by then. We had a 4:30 wakeup call—we needed to head back across the border to Hong Kong, then to the airport. I lay there naked. The dim light through the rice paper illuminated the plastic spring that held my locker key to my right ankle. The air was humid and dank, like stale, musty AC. I wasn't even sure if the investor was still across the hall. My passport was in a locker five floors below, along with my clothes. The RYNO was off somewhere again—who knew where this time? The plan was that the bike would be at the hostel in the morning. I would need to disassemble it, box it, and get it to the airport.

What is it about trust? How had I moved through this experience with such ease to this point? Did I suddenly become some sort of Zen master? Or was I that rare breed who was just equal parts stupid and lucky for one long, strange weekend in a foreign land? No matter what kind of logic I ran to soften the reality, I was seriously screwed in a massive way if that man wasn't sleeping across the hall.

All I knew was that I'd had a good feeling about the investor since we met weeks earlier. He had just left a high power job as a fast moving product launch director for a global consumer products company. He knew how to make shit happen, and clearly had a nice posse of dudes around him he could call on.

There was something transcendent about the next couple of hours. They drifted by as I rolled over all the decisions I had made up to that moment. Where had I miscalculated? What would I do differently next time? It was important for me to own my mistakes so I could learn from them.

While lying there, I reflected on how this new infusion of funding might be the kick we needed to get the bike into production.

The investor was convinced it was going to be easy: just like any product launch, show them some sketches, then do a lot of hand waving and yelling until they get it.

Something about that approach didn't sit well with me. Where I came from in the auto industry, we handed someone a drawing with a lot of tolerances on it, then demanded that we get back what we asked for.

I watched 4:30 slowly tick its way to the present, then rolled off the mattress, threw on my robe, and poked my head out the door. I whispered the investor's name and waited. After the third try, I heard a muffled voice answer—he needed another 20 minutes.

I went back in my room and listened to some shuffling and a soft female voice through the walls. A few minutes went by. Then I heard the investor.

"Let's go," he said.

PART 4:
MY EROTIC AWAKENING

As a boy I wanted to dance naked and be loved for it. Once I entered the harsh and mechanical world with my ego to protect me, I managed to keep that dream alive. I experimented with innovative creations, and remained transparent so others could build on my discoveries. Sharing them led me to realize it's not my ego, but my curiosity that gives me strength to perform the great heroic enactment of WHO I AM—a wild and precious dance that could not be performed in any way other than naked.

The Erotic Ball

Before I left my wife, I longed to rebuild my friendship network. I signed up for a few online groups, and one day received an email announcement for something called "The Erotic Ball." I mentioned it to Jean, sharing my curiosity about what it would be like to go. She was fine with it—she seemed open to me finding an outlet for my new interests. When I went online to buy tickets I was puzzled when I had to fill out an application questionnaire. I wrote something about wanting to rediscover my erotic self, hit "send," and forgot about it. A few weeks later, I received confirmation that I'd been accepted to attend.

When the night came, I dressed in the black motorcycle leathers I'd kept since high school, a black T-shirt, spiked my hair and went out the door. When I pulled up to the address, it was an old Grange Hall in North Portland. After snaking through a long line up the alley, I pushed through a narrow entry and looked out onto a huge wooden dance floor packed with a writhing, DJ driven crowd.

To the side of the floor was a private, partitioned-off section the size of about six phone booths. I later heard it was called "The Feel-out Booth." The walls had oval shaped, cloth-covered holes cut in them. A vertical slit in the fabric allowed people to anonymously reach in. Inside, people laughed and giggled at the thrill of unknown hands touching their bodies.

As the night went on, the space began to swell with men and women dressed in sexy costumes. I'm not talking simple sexy cocktail dresses, either. Women were dressed in the kind of sheer lace you'd see in the window of an adults-only shop—tits packaged and presented like fine pastries on white doilies. Men and women in handmade bondage gear, rocking corsets made from hickory branches and laced with ribbon. Dudes sporting silk pants, black leather shorts, and mesh T-shirts. Bare chests beneath white smoking jackets. Women leading men around by leashes, and vice versa. THIS was no general public Mardi Gras party.

As a married man, I was overwhelmed by the over-the-top magnitude of the wild bacchanalian cornucopia of flesh, glitter, and leather. Holy fuck! Had I been sleeping my entire 20-year marriage? I barely knew what I was looking at, let alone how to manage my desire to engage with these people, or how to be curious without being seen as a "creeper."

My scanning eyes landed on a gorgeous little belly dancer whose tiny hips gyrated in a wild, wide circle. When she caught my eyes with a sort of "Hi, I see you there" look, I was for some reason startled and looked away quickly. To her left stood an amazing lederhosen-clad woman I'll call Helga. She looked like she just stepped out of a Swiss milking barn. I awkwardly danced toward her, hypnotized by her huge, ice cream scoop boobs that heaved to the music's rhythm. Her eyes were closed. Lingering on that vertigo cleavage, her dancing almost made me lose my balance.

I circled around behind to see her big, Robert Crumb-style ass clad in tight leather booty shorts. A pair of telephone pole legs, with white knee-high stockings, sprung out from underneath. And those blonde pigtails on each side of her head—I wanted to run at her from behind, grab them and push her off a cliff like riding a dragon down a ravine then up into the heavens. What a woman!

I finally found a woman my age to dance with. She asked if I wanted to go downstairs and watch people having sex. We sat against a wall and looked out at a sea of futons and bodies. Once I adjusted to the novelty of it, the vibe was kind of sweet: the blend of different women's voices in their erotic bliss—so calming and life-affirming. Eventually, the woman said she had to go. We hugged respectfully, and I sat back down to steep in the vibe a bit longer.

After a while, I went back upstairs. The dance floor had emptied except for Helga and a guy she was talking to.

Checking in with my newly minted *inner impulsive instigator*, I walked up to her.

"Excuse me," I said, nodding toward the dude. I looked at Helga kindly and took a deep breath.

"Would you like to feel me up in the feel-out booth?"

Helga and the dude looked at each other for a second, puzzled. She looked at me with a shrug.

"Okay."

I turned and headed to the booth. Half way, I pivoted—they were still standing there talking. I held my arms out wide in an impatient *what the fuck* kind of stance.

"HEY!" I yelled.

Helga turned toward me, tilted her head, then jabbed her finger toward the booth.

"Get in there," she yelled back. "I'll be there in a second."

I stepped through the opening in the fabric. In the dim light, I could see I wasn't alone. The belly dancer from earlier was there, making out with two other women. I didn't care. I ripped my clothes off and waited for Helga.

Finally, a hand appeared through one of the openings—then another. I positioned myself so she could touch me. Her hands gently slid up the sides of my naked body, her fingers dancing lightly. One hand disappeared then reappeared through a lower opening to feel up and down my legs. It was pure sensory overload with a frothy thrill.

She brushed her fingers past my cock, lingered a little more each time she went by. She lifted my cock ever so lightly, gliding her fingers up and down its length with the fluttery touch of butterfly wings.

My cock began to stiffen.

"Come in here," I whispered.

"I can't." she countered.

"Why not?"

"I just can't."

"Then just come over by the door."

As her hands pulled away, I turned toward the door. Reaching into the darkness, I found myself ambushed by a pair of slippery, fat lips, kissing me passionately. Against my skin, I felt what I recognized as razor stubble.

I reached out to steady myself, and felt a narrow waist clad in a belly dancer's outfit—the same belly dancer I noticed earlier in the night. A shaft of light from a rotating spot light confirmed this was a dude.

I tried to wave him off.

"I'm busy," I said. I lunged toward Helga, who'd just appeared at the door. I locked eyes with her. Looking for her sign of approval, I stuck two fingers into her leather bustier. She arched her back approvingly. Seeing it as an invitation, I yanked her bustier down to expose a perfectly round breast. Just as I was about to lean in to press my lips onto her nipple, the belly dancer's mouth was on my hard cock.

My mind raced back over the evening. I'd seen him on the floor, thinking he was a woman—we held eyes until I looked away sheepishly. We'd kissed a moment ago. I hadn't exactly told to him to back off. That was as far as my logical brain could go before I returned to what my body knew: his mouth was still on my cock, his fists wringing it out like a dish-rag.

I realized pretty quickly this was no girly blowjob. This was a man's cock sucking.

My knees buckled as I rolled on my back to the floor. He had me, his iron grip trying to pull my cock out by the roots. Splayed on the floor, I steadied myself as his hand motion switched to a rattle-can wrist action—like a graffiti artist tagging in the shadows.

In the euphoria of that heightened erotic sensation, my mind flashed to thinking about the last time I tried to have sex with my wife. It was always a bit sad: *Why do you hide your erotic self from me? I restored this house for us and played it by the book. Why do you make me climb through this barbed wire to find you?*

Then I looked at the man in front of me. This vibrant belly dancer, with his sequined, coin-covered scarf—in his full erotic expression, modeling what the force of this creative drive felt like—fearlessly imposed his carnal pleasure on me.

His head lowered down, my throbbing cock extended deeper into his throat. A primal sound came out of him—the low hack of a lion. He lingered there, his mouth straining open, teeth cutting into my pelvis as he gagged out a long expulsion of air and fluid.

He lifted his head slowly. Long strings of mucus stretched to his upper lip. Time stopped as our eyes met. A deep sense of trust came over me as he reached over to pin my shoulder to the floor, then grabbed my cock with his other hand and started pumping.

He was smaller than me, but I could feel his power—like a brute driving a spike into a railroad tie. I thought to myself, *If I come now, I'm going to tear a fucking groin muscle.*

I slowed my excitement down by breathing, each exhale resonating from a deeper vibration in my throat.

Finally, I couldn't hold back. The involuntary contractions started to well up from a place deep in my spine, and spread across my stomach. I jack-knifed forward in a deep, spastic jerk, folding in half as my muscles clenched and squeezed. Almost passing out from the lack of air, the orgasm ripped through my body, lofting a huge load over my chest, landing in my left eye.

Blinded, I felt him pump me four more times, "Oh. My. Fucking. God." And then he was gone.

In that stillness, I reached for my t-shirt to wipe my face and chest. It was dead quiet. Everyone was gone. A feeling of peace came over me. I had no shame. For the first time in my life, I had not been the one driving.

From that place of surrender, I realized what it might be like for women to be in the vulnerable and courageous position of receiving and bearing whatever the momentum of an erotic enactment might be. It was eye-opening to recognize that, as an erotic encounter starts to unfold, it takes on a certain trajectory that a person can't always easily influence.

I had a newfound appreciation for ways that women can open to what is happening—their courage to stay in it, and the hopes it will turn out okay.

How many times had my own egoic drive into the fog of sex allowed me to get what I wanted without being fully aware of the isolating effect I might be having on my partner? Maybe I should start showing up with a new compassion for what's in it for both of us.

☼

Vulnerability is the very simple act of accepting ourselves, and one another, through sharing an experience that may be unique or new. Men and women relate with such nuance when they venture into the darkness together in conscious and consensual erotic play. No matter the path, when we open our eyes to see the other person, we find out more about ourselves, and lead our partners and ourselves closer to an embodied wholeness.

Once the clutter of self-doubt clears like a raging fire through the underbrush, and the shame of not being allowed to express one's own sexuality has been chased out of the forest, the time to listen to our own erotic awakening arrives. Claiming our erotic expression is perhaps our most liberating act of rebellion. By claiming our freedom to embody whatever consensual erotic inspiration we are called to feel, we break from the confines of a culture that tries to control us through shame. When we become transparent in who we are as sexual creatures, we offer our leadership to help others claim *their* unique erotic expression.

We cannot claim the fullness of who we are until we allow others to voice the fullness of who *they* are. The belly dancer showed me one of my earliest and most powerful initiations into vulnerability. He revealed himself to me; he knew I could have judged him, or kept my erotic expression to myself. He took a chance, and through his lead I was forever awakened to the full spectrum of our erotic animal natures. We accepted one another in that moment, and began living as people who are already free.

Normal Boyfriend Behavior

After a while, I managed to get through enough awkward casual sexual encounters to feel like I knew what I was doing again. It was odd though—I was so much more mature as an adult, but I still found myself a bit overwhelmed trying to create an authentic connection. Whenever that happened, a performance anxiety would come up, and I'd go back to a conventional adolescent lovemaking style that relied on the objectification of women to get sexually turned-on. It took a while to realize the underlying mechanism in play.

I would look at a woman as being the object that turned me on, and then get confused when she wasn't sexy enough. What I discovered was that I had all kinds of shame in claiming my right to feel sexy, or be turned on for my own erotic reasons. I struggled with this realization. Even as I tried to find my own erotic response, things got worse. When I focused on performance, I would leave myself open to the fear of judgment—how *good* was the performance? And with this came a second fear: of me being judgmental of others to level the playing field.

During this awkward time, I met a woman from Seattle named Ingred. She and I were in the same group at a conference on building healthy relationship skills. She carried herself with a certain type of maturity, both intellectually and physically, moving in an embodied sort of way.

Luck had it that there was a little diner next to the conference center where I found myself sitting at a table with her. I felt an attraction right away. She was lilty and funny, but also had an intensity to her. And she definitely had an opinion about the way she saw things.

After the conference was over, we emailed and talked on phone for a few weeks. Finally, she invited me up to her place in Seattle. I was enthralled by her, and also had a deep respect for the caliber of woman she was. Imagining what I was about to walk into, I contacted my therapist friend and asked her how I should handle myself with Ingrid in her most private space.

"How do I move confidently into her bedroom, but at the same time show that I fully respect her?" I asked.

"If you find yourself in her bedroom," she said, "make sure and ask permission before you climb into her bed."

After being out all afternoon, Ingred and I ended up in her little front parlor. Just as our conversation started to trail off, she said, "Let's go in my room." She tilted her head to motion for me to follow her.

When she opened the door, I peered into the most gorgeous yet classically feminine bedroom I'd ever seen. Soft gauzy curtains framed the windows on the far wall. A huge tapestry ran up the wall behind her headboard, and looped out over the bed to form a canopy of sorts. Candles hung over every horizontal surface. Fuzzy throw rugs on both sides of the bed insulated against the cold hardwoods.

Ingrid calmly began taking her clothes off, then neatly folded them on her nightstand. The way the evening light fell on her soft skin, and the ease and fluid motion of her body completely hypnotized me. As you can imagine, I had my clothes off pretty quickly, then lingered and watched her. Had I not been coached ahead of time, I may have jumped straight into her bed and smiled back at her like "This is awesome!"

It was so perfect to just stand there quietly, then ask if I could enter her bed—and then to have her smile so wide and gesture for me to do so. I climbed up and pulled the sheet aside for her to slide into my waiting arms.

As this first erotic encounter hit its stride, I kept drifting off in my head—the whole thing was such a trip, the little voices in my head questioning my performance, even while I was physically *there*.

"Where did you go?" she asked me. She could sense I was gone somewhere, not fully present. She called me back by saying, "I can't feel you." When she did, she invited me to return to my body and stay in the moment with her.

I slowed down, and learned to pay more attention to what was happening in the room. My ability to connect with her became part of a larger expression that moved our connection from a monologue to a conversation.

☼

The last time I went to see Ingred in Seattle, she got me at the airport in her little mini-pickup. It had a throaty exhaust leak that bugged the crap out of me.

Ingrid was chatty, started venting about how all the guys she tried to date in Seattle were too fixated on collaboration. According to her, they always *needed* her opinion on the most mundane things.

"Why can't guys just make fucking decisions on their own," she lamented at one point.

That afternoon, I dropped her at work, and had the truck for the whole day. When I returned to her apartment, I crawled under it, and found the exhaust leak—a hole in the side of the muffler. I went to the hardware store, bought a piece of sheet aluminum and a few hose clamps, installed it, and the noise was gone. That night, I casually told her I fixed the leak.

"That's amazing," she said. "You mean guys just do that?"

"I don't know what kind of guys you've been hanging out with," I replied, "but where I'm from, that's normal boyfriend behavior." She squinted and trailed off into her thoughts.

The next morning, we had to catch my early flight. The alarm went off. She reached over to kill it, then slid her hand down my leg and grabbed my cock, which happened to be half-hard. She threw the covers back, and went down on me to get it nice and ready. Then she climbed up and wiggled her pussy down on it. She leaned forward, looked me straight in the eyes and began lifting and rolling her hips in a decisive *milking me* motion, then pounded up and down a few times. It was only a minute or two before she stopped, casually climbed off and chirped, "Come on, we have to get going."

"What the FUCK was THAAAT?" I demanded.

"I don't know what kind of women you've been hanging out with," she joked, "but for me, that's normal girlfriend behavior."

Not long after, Ingrid's life took a detour. She moved back to the East Coast, and we drifted out of contact. But the feeling of being with her has stuck with me.

She modeled a new approach to connection. Through her, something began coming alive in me. I saw a new path forward. No longer did I enter into a sexual encounter from a big energy, make-out-grope-a-thon place. Instead, I brought with me the intention of connecting from a quiet foundation of consent: to just *be there* in a way that felt collaborative. This quiet peace created a more intimate platform from where we could ramp our sexuality up together. I was amazed at how passionate and animalistic the love-making could become, having begun so quietly.

I believe the goal in intimacy is to work toward a place where each person trusts the other enough to relax their defenses. In the middle of a state of acceptance comes the courage to rebel against our own shame in a container we find safe.

The awkward part for me: in this new co-creational way of connecting with women, I found myself in a no-man's land between an objectification-driven sex drive, and a growing capacity for a true heart-felt collaboration. In other words, I watched myself letting go of my egoic attachment to how I thought sex *should be.* I learned to shut up, slow *waaaaay* down, and be radically present to what we were creating together. As a result, I let go of the need to use sexual performance to mask my fear. By opening myself up to being seen, even in my vulnerability, I replaced the fear of the unknown with a dedication to create an authentic connection.

In a nutshell, I unplugged my cock from my ego, and plugged it into my heart.

During this "rewiring process," there were times when I lost track of where my erection went. It was terrifying, but in the end, I was actually giving my erection permission to show up if it wanted to. I took the time to explain to the woman I was with that I was moving through a new approach to sexual connection, claiming my own right to feel sexy without looking to her to turn me on. I wanted my partner to understand that no matter what state my cock was in, it was never tied to my feelings of desire for her.

The process proved pivotal for me. My sexual enjoyment went from a tepid *job to do,* to an improvisational, joy-filled, full-tilt rock opera.

The second thing that blew me away during this era: I was creating an invitation for my partner. Instead of worrying about *turning me on*, she could bring her whole creative, erotic expression to bear, including her vulnerability—and what she would share in this space was far more amazing and sophisticated than I could have ever imagined.

Boundaries

Once RYNO Motors was funded and we had a full staff, I moved into a nice two-bedroom apartment downtown, and threw a big party to celebrate a new phase in my life. I called it the "Pause Party," and invited all my friends with the intention to just pause our lives for one night.

One of the women who showed up was Brenda, someone I'd been having occasional but highly physical energetic dances with for years. She had a unique capacity to open a deep sensual channel on the dance floor, but off the floor she was an introvert—kept her private life to herself.

Brenda wore a gorgeous red flowing dress. As the host, I hardly had a chance to talk with her, but as she was leaving, she handed me a CD with a playlist of songs she'd burned. I was deeply touched and told her I would listen to it the next day.

On the way to work the next morning, I stuck it in the CD player and drove. My car was suddenly filled with the most ethereal, passionate music I had ever heard. It completely took me by surprise. Who would share such vulnerability and know I would understand its meaning? I called to thank her, and shared how much her playlist moved me. As we spoke, I could feel a natural opening forming. These kinds of openings come and go between friends, but this one had a vibrancy to it. I gathered the courage to ask her if she would dance alone with me to her mix. I held my breath and waited.

"I would enjoy that," she replied.

I asked a good friend who owned a yoga studio if I could use his space after hours. He agreed and gave me the door code. A few days later, Brenda and I met out front, went inside, and changed into our dance clothes. We put the CD into the player, but before she hit play she looked over at me, her eyes asking *now what?*

We stood facing one other for a moment.

"We should talk about boundaries," I suggested.

Anticipating how quickly this encounter could move, and with all the classes I'd taken on consent and boundaries, I was keen to make sure we talked this out.

Brenda looked to me to make the first suggestion.

"Is erotic touch okay," I asked. "Can I run my hands over your body? Do you have any off-limit areas?"

She took a breath.

"I have a sense I'm going to struggle with boundaries tonight."

"Can we get naked?"

"Yes."

We both knew boundaries can stretch as wide or as tight as one wants to set them. But no matter their shape or scope, any boundary with a defined limit is better than one that's fuzzy or unclear. A clear boundary allows you to run right up and spear yourself all over it if you like, but never cross the line. With good, hard boundaries, people stay in their bodies; they don't disappear into their heads, watching for a misstep, or trying to manage a frontier of unknowns. I shared this concept with Brenda, and she agreed.

"I'm keeping intercourse off the table," I said.

"I respect that," she replied.

I reached over and clicked the play button.

As the first songs went by, I began to sense how open and languid the energy between us was. I'd never experienced a dance this sultry. We had plenty of time, and allowed our movements to unfold in an ancient, instinctual courtship dance.

Midway through the CD, the song rising into a crescendo, we started to tear each other's clothes off. We smashed our bare chests together. I lifted Brenda in my arms and slowly carried her in a wide arc before gently setting her down on her tiptoes.

Dancing with a woman when you're free to run your hands all over her naked body is like creating a work of art with your fingertips—smearing the viscous paint, feeling the tug of the canvas. There's a certain poise to it. It inspires even greater respect, consciousness, and reverence than when dancers are clothed.

For two hours we explored an immersive, erotic mystery. At one moment, we found each other rolling on the floor—the music must have stopped. How long had we been dancing in silence, completely in tune with our own inner rhythm?

We composed ourselves in a funny pantomime, almost like someone had walked in on us. We dressed deliberately and walked outside. On the stoop, we held each other in a tender embrace and agreed to meet again.

For the next four months, we met nearly every other week. I'd go to her half-furnished apartment. She'd make us a salad, and spread a wide sheet in the middle of the empty carpeted living room floor. She'd put on her latest selection of music, and we'd dance together—each time we'd end up on her floor again.

Our ritual of finding each other evolved into a tribal, visceral encounter with an intellectual sizzle running up over the top of it. We didn't just roll around together and start kissing—we tore at each other's skin, and drank the other's blood.

Sometimes we were slow, deep, and penetrating. Sometimes we rode down tumbling rivers of ecstasy together. We explored underworlds, sensations, and movements of our bodies, punctuated by tempests of animal abandon. Of all the women I'd been with to that point, Brenda was by far the most confident—always in touch with her emotions through such a variety of heightened states of being. What a thrill to be a part of this level of sexual expression and desire.

Between each round, we'd lie on the floor, reflect on what we'd just experienced, and share how we'd felt throughout the encounter. We were always amazed at how our individual experiences were so aligned and in-sync. There was a simple feeling of joy and companionship between us—we were inventing life as we went along.

As the months carried on, we started to realize that there was no real relationship framework for our erotic explorations. Brenda was clear about not wanting to be in a relationship—she had just ended one. I was clear for similar reasons.

The night we finally talked about it, everything shifted. With no framework to hold us, our deepening connection felt destabilizing. Not being at a place in our lives to build one, we had no choice but to stop seeing each other. We handled it with grace and kindness toward one another—no guilt trip, not an ounce of trying to control things. We just let go.

There's nothing wrong with consenting adults engaging in erotic play, and seeing how far the play will take them. However, we have to pay attention to what we're playing with, stay honest about our motivations, and keep a sense of where we think we're going.

Brenda and I retained an obligation to be honest with one another in what we wanted from our encounters. This is basic respect. Talking about boundaries early is always a good thing, especially once it becomes clear from the chemistry between two people that it's game-on.

A safe sex conversation, for instance, goes well beyond discussing fluids. It includes getting to the bottom of why you're fucking, what you expect from it, what level of commitment you're at, and where you are on the fuck-yes scale. Then you match your energy to your understanding of the other person. The last thing a man should do is give a woman a big fat soul fucking when she's not ready or interested in receiving it.

Mac-and-Cheese

I opened up a chat on OkCupid with a woman named Jessy. Our dialogue was going great from the start. She was super witty, had a successful online business, and right away wanted to meet at a motorcycle museum/coffee house.

An hour before I was to leave to meet her, she texted to say she couldn't do it. I asked why not. She said she was crying, was a total mess, and hadn't even started to put on her makeup. I asked what the deal was. She said she felt like a total impostor, and that she was in no shape to date or even get over what she was going through.

I told her to call me. She wouldn't, just kept texting what was going on for her. I texted her back, "Just call me!" She finally did.

"How about I just come over," I said. "We can drink whisky, and you can get pissed off about whatever's going on."

She agreed, and texted me her address. I grabbed a fifth off the counter, and headed out.

When she swung the door open, what I saw was a tall, thin woman, her hair a total mess, and her eyes bloodshot and puffy. I have no idea how she had the courage to invite me over. Maybe it had been a while since someone offered her the thoughtful attention I gave her, or asked her the kinds of questions I was asking.

We sat in her living room. She talked and sobbed, sobbed and talked. I poured out small boosters of whisky. She told me about being a trained ballerina, how she met an abusive guy who talked her into moving to

Turkey for five years, and made her wear a Burka. She got pregnant, left the guy, and managed to get out of the country. After that she spent a year hopping between friends' houses before she found this place. Boiled all the way down, she was a highly distraught woman who'd described herself in her profile as being a put-together, hip, potential great date.

I listened the whole way through, and reflected back to her everything she said. When she finally calmed down, I asked if she wanted to get out of there to clear the air.

"I know a nice little bar that does an awesome mac-and-cheese."

"That would be great!" she said.

We sat on the back patio of the bar. The mac-and-cheese had its expected calming effect, and she slowly relaxed. To offer some insight into what she'd been through, I shared my philosophy about setting boundaries, asking for what you want, and offering only what you are comfortable to offer in exchange for what you asked for.

"The idea," I said, "is to free yourself to only sign up for what you want to offer, then be unattached to whether the other person thinks it's worth it."

Jessy was curious about how all that worked. I shared stories from a few recent encounters that had been uncomplicated, simple, and fun.

"A person can share the absolute minimum of what they want to offer," I said. "The invitation doesn't have to take anyone's needs into account but your own. Then the other person is free to decide whether or not he or she wants to engage."

"So," she started, "if I like someone but I don't want to get too involved right away, I can just ask for something simple to get to the next step?"

"Yes! The goal is to not get overwhelmed by it, or talk yourself out of doing any of it. You decide the size of the next step, no matter how very small."

She went quiet as I was signing the check.

"You want to go?" she asked.

As I drove Jessy home, she stared out the window. Then out of nowhere she said, "I don't know what you did, but my pussy is gushing wet right now. I haven't been this wet in years."

It took me a minute, but I said with an affirming chuckle, "Well that sums up nicely how the evening is going." She totally got it. She smiled.

"Thank you for being so honest," I added.

She remained quiet the rest of the way—not distant, but introspective for sure. I clicked the car into park when we reached her house, the motor still running.

She turned to me abruptly.

"Okay," she said. "You want to hear what my minimum desire is to move this thing forward?"

"Go for it."

"You can fuck me on the stairs. No touching me above the waist because of all my shame from wearing a Burka. Just pull my pants down, get your cock out, and fuck me from behind."

I paused for a moment looking at her. I felt really proud of her for naming what she wanted, but to be honest, the image of that act terrified me. It's one thing to have a female acquaintance, someone you already know, call you up when things are rough and ask if you'll just come over for a consensual romp. It's a completely different situation to seduce a woman, whether knowingly or not, who's clearly struggling with her emotional state.

"I'm going to let this one go," I said. "I'm not sure if you're wasted or not."

"I'm not wasted," she said, and slid out of the car. Then she turned around and poked her head in through the window.

"Thanks for the great night," she said. "You really picked me up."

I drove away. A few blocks later I got a text from her.

"Do you have any condoms with you?"

I went home and thought about Jessy for a while. Who knows—maybe I should have taken her up on her offer. The more I thought about her, the more I realized just how courageous it was for her to share her fears and insecurities with me. I could have done the same and shared my fear of meeting her on the stairs.

I've talked to plenty of women who say that when a man fails to share his fears, they just get sad. They feel like he doesn't trust them, or that he's just driving forward into the void without including her, even when they're in the middle of making love.

Saying something vulnerable is an offering that gives someone else a chance to show up as they are, regardless of whether they want to love or abandon us. To walk that line—to truly go there and reveal ourselves in front of another person . . . that's courage.

Just Three Hours Once a Week

Not long after I left my marriage, I rented a room in a big community house. I didn't go out much, but would occasionally meet women at potlucks, some of whom I knew from dance. When I heard that certain women were asking around about me, I felt confident my street cred in the community was solid.

I wasn't in any emotional shape to be in a new relationship. I was still going back to my old house to work with Jean and get it ready for the market. Being so new to the dating scene, I would often become overwhelmed by how to present or *sell* myself. It didn't take long to realize I may as well just be radically honest. A man is more worthy of a woman's trust when he isn't trying a hard-sell, or offering more than he can deliver. It's like, "Hey, listen, I can only offer this much of myself," or, "I'm not even officially divorced yet, do you still want to get together?"

During this time, I experimented with different ways to interact with women and create invitations to spend time together. As I refined my skills, I discovered how important it was to be unattached to receiving a "no," remembering that the answer wasn't about *me*, but about their boundaries, experiences, and needs.

Many women I chatted with at parties shared that they weren't ready for dating. "Things are complicated," they'd explain, or they had issues with past loves, family, or just didn't have the time.

During this period, I continued to refine my capacity to ask for what I wanted, shut up, and let whatever was going to happen just happen. Eventually, I became more confident and bold. In a moment of either a lapse in judgment or pure inspiration, I asked a woman in a calm voice, "You want to just come over for three hours once a week?"

"What would that entail?" she asked.

"Here's the deal," I clarified. "No text messages, no phone calls, no email. It's not a relationship. It's just three hours on an afternoon, once a week."

"That sounds interesting," she replied. Her eyes brightened. "What would we do?"

"I don't know. Lie on my bed and look out the window, or read a book to each other, or tell stories. Or I could slowly trace an ice cube up your spine."

There was a long pause.

"I could do that," she said.

It must have been beginner's luck: three women enthusiastically agreed to come and go that summer. There was intentionally no pressure, escalation, or promise of anything other than being open to what was alive between us. It was nothing more complicated than, "Can we simply just enjoy one other?" The agreement was based on mutual honesty and clear communications from the start.

☼

Betty was one of the women who agreed to my proposal. She only came by once, but radically changed my perspective on a certain type of erotic experience women sometimes seek.

Betty seemed purposeful. She was voluptuous, a well put-together, professional voice teacher who was both open and direct. The day she came over, I walked her upstairs to my room, and asked her what had inspired her to show up.

"I like you," she said. "You seem confident in who you are. To be honest though, I'm not really interested in looking out the window or telling stories."

"So you're more of an 'ice cube' date?"

Her expression didn't change.

"Have you ever had your cock sucked by a dominant woman?" she asked.

"Umm, maybe not?" was the best I could come back with.

"Sit down," she said. She pointed to the edge of the bed.

She knelt down in front of me and matter-of-factly unzipped and pulled off my pants. She took my flaccid cock in her fist and pulled it straight out tight with a jerk. She grabbed a hefty pinch of my scrotum and pulled down just as firmly.

"I don't want your little pleasure-hungry penis," she said. "I want you to bring me your big, fat, manly cock."

She leaned into me, then slowly and deliberately lowered her open mouth over the head of my cock. The combination of subtle pain and warm wetness made my toes start to curl. My cock started responding quickly as she pulled again firmly on my sack. She took more of me into her mouth as I grew harder. I resisted groaning out loud as she stopped and looked up.

"Now imagine your cock connected to the base of your spine," she said. "Fill your cock with the man you are and hold your power still."

I leaned back, held up my fists, pulled my arms wide and tightened my pecs across my chest. My whole body was taut and rigid as Betty fervently twisted and pulled my package. As my cock expanded, she took its entire length down her throat, wrapped her arms around my ass, and then in a long, expressive gesture, bowed her head down. She lingered there, slightly gagging before lifting her head slowly, one hand clenched around my shaft. I didn't touch her. Remembering what I'd learned from Magdalena the Tantrika, I sensed Betty didn't need me to initiate or respond with a reciprocal cycle of pleasure or erotic dialogue.

Betty was provoking a visceral feeling in me that I had a hard time making sense of. As she gave my cock another fierce tug, she was showing me something I had never experienced. She had no interest in my desire to be stroked into a conventional, tactile orgasm. Through her intense physicality and forcefulness, she demanded my whole self and willpower to throw off judgement of what this looked like.

There's an erotic frontier when a woman can summon her own strength, and demand that a man meets her where she wants him to be. When a man consciously contains his desire for pleasure, he offers his erotic partner the gift of her own power—she will take his cock on *her* terms, not the other way around.

In this dynamic, the man must still hold onto his masculine presence, and be a foundation for her pleasure—without inflicting his own needs into the encounter.

This type of erotic play is different than when a man takes on a submissive role during the act of receiving. Instead, a man in his masculine power, even while surrendering, gives his partner an axis point from where she can feel herself, and her own power. In that way, it's not about power meeting submissiveness, but about power meeting power, trust meeting trust.

There are many times when a woman looks for a hard, directed thing to hold on to, both metaphorically and literally. In that form of masculine expression, a man needs to be solid and unattached to his inherent need to please, or his need for a specific kind of pleasure. The embodied woman, fully in her power, knows what she needs to enact. She can find it on her own.

※

Betty and I sourced our power from one another along the channel our bodies formed. She wanted a symbolic pillar of strength—something she could literally climb onto and trust that it would hold her as she dropped her defenses and descended into something deep and primal.

Her grabbing and owning my cock like this wasn't about *my* enjoyment—it was about Betty using my hard cock as an anchor. What she needed from me—and what I gave her—was the physical and energetic support that protected her experience.

She became completely and utterly self-absorbed in her own cock pleasure. I was with her the whole time, holding my position like a thick stone dike against a heaving ocean.

As the encounter escalated, Betty ripped her shirt and bra off like they were on fire. Her hair danced wildly on her bare shoulders. She pulled a thin belt out from her unbuckled pants and wrapped it around the base of my shaft and balls, cinched it tight, and tugged on it rhythmically as she sucked.

I had to grab a pillow to cover my mouth as I yelled out—an intense mix of pain and pleasure like nothing I'd ever felt. I held my ground for Betty, all while experiencing a version of my cock I'd never known before. It was the first time a woman wasn't trying to please me, but actually wanted to feel *herself* through my cock.

Finally, a roar came out of me—I was *here* in this moment, meeting the desire of such a powerful woman. What a sense of arrival for us both.

When she was done, Betty slid up on top of me. I held her in a lingering embrace that contained a deep and unspoken understanding of one other. I could feel her body uncoil—like a woman who'd been swimming against an ocean's rip tide for hours and had finally crawled onto the beach. The world stopped for us. Everything was a quiet bliss.

As her breath calmed, she finally rolled off, put on her shirt, stuffed her bra in her purse and looked at me.

"I should probably go," she said. "If we try to talk about what just happened, we'll be here forever."

What we'd just created was still alive in the room. I wanted us to bask in its light a bit longer. I didn't know whether I should start talking, or just stand quietly with her. I finally managed to stumble some words out.

"Umm ... that was a lot," I said. "I mean…beautiful…intense…I might need some time, you know." I was stammering, stuck in a combination of wanting to hold her and wanting to hide my inability to meet her in such honest, exposed vulnerability.

After a long pause, Betty turned and walked to the door.

"Thank you for that," she said. Then she left.

In our male dominated culture, when a woman knows how to embody her full self, and take her rightful position of power with a man, it can be startling. I'm not talking about her desire to dominate, but quite the opposite: her right to exist at the same influence and engagement level.

As men, we have an inherited and socially sanctioned confidence in our superiority. We unconsciously walk among women who walk around us. Betty let me know clearly what she was "made of," and gave me the gift of making sure I could feel it. This whole exchange woke me up to wondering just how disengaged women are from men, simply from the exhaustion of trying to reach us.

Second Tantrika Visit

As my marriage declined in intimacy, my wife and I tried going out to dinner more often. There was so much hidden anger between us, it was almost impossible to relax and feel anything that resembled a flow or spontaneity. After an especially disheartening evening, I thought I might go back to Magdalena the Tantrika for some personal work.

After scheduling a session, I drove over to her quiet street and sat in my car for a bit, trying to figure out why I felt so disconnected from myself. Nothing was coming to mind, so I just went to her door and rang the bell.

We walked up to her little sitting area, where she asked me what I needed.

"I think I have some anger issues with women," I said, surprised to hear the words come out of my mouth.

"Hmm," she said. "What kind of anger?"

"I feel controlled by women. I don't know how to feel accepted by them, or how to fully trust them. I always feel a subtle yank on my choke chain."

We talked for a few more minutes. Then she motioned for me to join her on the futon and sit upright on the bed with her, face-to-face. Both wearing sarongs, she positioned us with our legs intertwined—*Yab-Yum*, in Tantric lingo.

Without saying a word, she pulled her colorful sarong down around her waist to expose her bare breasts. She cupped them, bounced them in front of me, and ran her fingers slowly through her hair, flaunting her sexiness.

"Okay Chris," she said. "Here I am, the canvas that men normally project their objectification onto. Put both your arms around me," she went on. "Touch the middle of my spine at my shoulder blades with your fingertips. Look me in the eyes. I want you to face and respect a woman in her beauty. Each time I feel like you respect me a bit more, I'll allow you to lower your hands two inches at a time, until you come to the tip of my tailbone."

Okay, that sounded like fun. I lowered my gaze to look her in the eyes, but rather than respect, what took off in my mind was rage.

"Who the fuck are you?" I heard in my head. "I think you're pretty sexy, so why don't you respond to me? Oh, you're not going to respond? Why, because you think you're some sexy, self-proclaimed Tantrika? Who are you to tell me how to feel and what to think? I'm the one who should be in charge here. It's your job to respond to *me*. Maybe being a bit angry is okay. Nice tits. What am I doing here anyway? This is so fucking stupid. How is this going to help me calm down? What a waste of time. You probably have no idea how important I am. Why should I have to wait for you to tell me what I can and cannot do?"

When I was 14, my family was on the way to our summer cabin when we stopped at my mom's coworker's wooded property. We had been invited to eat lunch, and to spend the afternoon touring the fire trails that led through his 40-acre parcel of forest. When he greeted us, he was with a younger woman named Pam, probably in her early 30s. I was instantly captivated—dressed in shorts and a tight bikini top, she was sexy, athletic, gorgeous…the perfect picture of objectification for a teenage boy.

My mom and dad headed to the cabin. Pam offered to drive us kids through the forest fire trails in an old restored Willys Jeep. She jumped behind the wheel with a bounce. I slid in the passenger seat, while my sister and brother hopped in the back.

Pam was kind and really funny. She laughed disarmingly every time her flip-flop clad foot slipped off the clutch pedal, stalling the motor.

As we jostled along the trails, I was transfixed by her heaving breasts that stretched the straps of her bikini top. With a hint of nipple showing, she shifted through the gears, jabbing her right arm forward and back, again and again. On the forward motion, her arm squished the side of her breast; pulling the shift lever back, her elbow would bump my upper arm. The repeated light physical contact was euphoric and highly erotic.

Her eyes were usually focused on the trail, which allowed me to gaze down at as much of her body as I could take in. I was mesmerized by her fleshy, animated show. After a few big bumps with her laughing out loud, I swore her boobs were going to fly right out of her top. Punctuated by her elbow's touch, the hair on my arm stood on end. It was all I could do to stay calm, push the bulge down in my shorts, and continue our small talk. Now and then she'd look over and smile. She was completely at peace with the situation, and comfortable in her body.

It was one of the first erotically charged experiences I ever had with a woman.

Our tour ended back at the cabin. When we all piled out of the jeep, I thanked Pam, then joined my parents. Standing next to my mom, I looked over at Pam one last time. She stood quietly in a shaft of sunlight, a vision of pure sexy. My mom looked at her too. Then she turned to me.

"You know she's a stripper, don't you?" was all she said.

My mom was an intellectual, a writer, and a creative force who started a few businesses through a network of professionals. I didn't really know how to challenge her comment.

Granted, it wasn't my mom's responsibility to protect me, or to be curious about my experiences. Boys go through initiations, whether moms are around or not. All mothers struggle with knowing when to let go and allow boys to make their own choices. Looking back on it today, I still suspect that my mom needed to sabotage my experience and devalue Pam so she didn't have to feel her own perceived inadequacy.

A confusing sense of fear shot through me. At that age, I was just opening up and learning to accept myself and women as sexual beings. After my mom spoke those words, I was afraid of what women might be hiding. My adolescent thoughts ran rampant. If it was so important for me to know that Pam was a stripper, why didn't she tell me herself? Was she hiding it? Did she lie to me by not telling me? Are strippers a unique class of people? Why had she been singled out? What about the sexy feelings in the jeep? Had she tricked me into feeling this way?

Tragically, as boys we learn to choke down these messages, and average them into all the other negative information we take in about women over time. As awakening men, it's our responsibility to strip this hardwiring out of our systems.

I struggled with Magdalena for 20 minutes. The whole time I was denigrating her in my head, I kept searching for some form of approval from her. By her unwavering stare, she implied she wasn't feeling it.

I cycled through all forms of fear about not being good enough, or not trusting powerful women. Finally, I went back to our first meeting, where we exchanged those memorable words: *I respect your place on this planet.*

Slowly, I started to soften. I could feel myself gradually accepting aspects of her and her path through life as a woman—the complexities of who she was, and all that was required of her to arrive in this moment. I finally let go of my mind's judgmental stories. I took a deep breath, let my chest fold a bit, and began to *see* her for the first time.

"There it is," she whispered. "Drop your hands two inches."

We did this for another half hour. I slowly worked my way down, one revelation at a time, letting go of one more story, discovering one more layer of connection with the person she truly was. I made it all the way down until my fingertips came to rest on her lower back.

She leaned forward and held me close. I was quiet, almost dumbfounded. No tears came over me, but a deep sense of peace set in. In the tranquility of that moment, her body felt inviting and soft, completely non-threatening. I realized I was no longer afraid of her—such a strange thing to feel, considering how unconscious I'd been to the fear. The contrast was revealing.

It takes a profound level of surrender to feel what we have been carrying. The surrender in this case wasn't to her, but to my ability to recognize how my anger was getting in the way of authentically seeing her.

In surrendering, I also chose to take responsibility for my own right to exist on this planet.

My gentle embrace was all I could do to thank her for the beauty she shared with me. I finally leaned back on my hands to gaze at her with newfound compassion. What I saw was not a projection screen anymore, but a woman smiling back at me. She looked younger for some reason, a vibrancy I must have missed.

Walking out her door, a *what the hell just happened* feeling came over me. Hours earlier, I couldn't even make contact with my issue. I knew

I was harboring anger, but didn't know the source. Where did my deep distrust come from? Eventually, I came to understand that it stemmed from being around women who didn't want to be intimate with me—from my mom, who couldn't even hug me when I was a kid, to my ex-wife, who couldn't trust her own intimacy, let alone share it with me.

To satisfy my unresolved need for intimacy, I kept seeking out any form of connection. Whenever I'd get put off enough, a sort of *fuck you* attitude came over me. I'd find myself saying something like, "I didn't want your intimacy in the first place."

What I needed was to allow myself to be seen in my *natural* state, and then challenge myself to look at women in an authentic way without judgment or projection. First, I had to find women that *had* a capacity for intimacy; then I had to learn to surrender and be vulnerable enough to be available. This awareness would eventually form a greater understanding and foundation of a magical new trust and connection.

☼

This whole notion of projection on women started by outsourcing my own erotic drive.

It was fascinating to have the opportunity, through Magdalena, to unplug one unconscious aspect at a time from my male psyche. I began to see how each one interacted with the others, and how they corresponded as a group.

When I hijacked the visual image of a woman to turn me on, whether or not she liked it, or even knew it, I wasn't owning my own erotic expression. When I projected my need to feel sexy onto a woman, and the effect wasn't heightened enough, I'd blame her, or would judge her by some sort of sexual currency—not *hot enough*, not *sexy enough*. I believed that by doing so, I was distancing myself from the woman, and blaming her for not finding me.

When men abandon their responsibility to own their erotic awareness, women find it not only unattractive, but sad. Worse, some women will poke back at a man for making her feel undervalued. I wonder if that's where my anger came from: not only was I putting all the pressure on women to turn *me* on, but I wound up feeling hurt, and even hating women for not reaching me in *my place* of need.

When a man offers a woman something he considers to be a compliment—even if he's simply evaluating her attractiveness—a woman may see this as judgment, creating distance between them. However, if a man comes from a place of leadership, and shares his true feelings about how his inner eroticism was inspired by something he found uniquely attractive in *himself* as a result of her vibrancy, she has something positive to respond to with an invitation for connection.

When men outsource their need to feel sexy, it's like handing your car keys over to someone, then critiquing the way they drive. Eventually it becomes a pure power struggle.

These dynamics aren't exclusive to males. The roles can be reversed. In fact, I bet we've all done this on some level in the past.

I used to think my partner was yanking on my choker collar. When I unpack that thought now, I see that I was actually allowing myself to be yanked, while openly handing her the leash.

As men, if we stand confidently in our right to feel as sexy as we want to—whether big or small—and leave our partner to be who she really is, we create a relationship dynamic that comes much closer to respecting each other's right to exist. Then, when we come together as couples, we do so from a place of potent, respectful, collaborative connection.

PART 5:
FREE NAVIGATION

The best we can do is look at our options, ask ourselves who we are now, then choose. I believe there is always only one choice: that which makes sense with the information we have, measured against our self-awareness. Once we make our choice, we have to take action and thrust ourselves into the unknown. The wake that ripples behind us is the physical signature of a world forever changed. In that wake is where our choices mix with the wake of others who have come before us. When we see life as a series of choices that lead us closer to freedom, why not choose boldly? All we have to lose is our comfort.

Punked in Stockholm

On our seventh date, Gillian met me at the airport in Stockholm. To promote the RYNO bike, I was starting a two-week speaking tour through Stockholm, Wolfsburg, and Berlin. She'd been on business travel already for a week. My flight to Stockholm was delayed. By the time I arrived and met her, she'd been musing on the fact that we hadn't had sex yet, and figured I'd punked her into buying a random ticket to Europe.

On the surface, she was a practicing Jungian oriented psychotherapist. Underneath, she was an ex-media producer who'd worked for a few big LA advertising agencies, but left because she no longer wanted such a yang lifestyle. In her true nature, she was this quiet-yet-wild creature from the hinterlands, one foot in the underworld, one in the real.

In the six weeks since our first date, I was still getting to know her, and refining my ability to contain her wild erotic wanderings. She loved how I could keep her energy from flying out into the bedroom by holding her legs, wrapping my arms around her shoulders, and pressing my chest down on her. We'd penetrated each other emotionally and spiritually, but not yet physically.

It's funny how opportunities lead to other opportunities we know nothing about at the time. If it wasn't for a San Francisco TED Talk, where producers wanted to use the RYNO as eye candy, I wouldn't have even been invited on stage. When the producer of the Stockholm speaking tour found my talk on YouTube, he reached out and invited me to Sweden.

My first gig was at the five-star Grand Hotel in Stockholm, right on the harbor across from the Royal Palace—a stunning example of French-style architecture steeped in Old World grace. They wanted me to present for 90 minutes in the main ballroom on the theme of innovation. The audience of about 200 high-net-worth investors would hear the RYNO story, complete with a secret reveal in the middle of the show—an operational RYNO bike. After the first show, Gillian and I would be free to wander across Sweden for 10 days until my next gig in Wolfsburg, Germany.

From an idea my daughter threw at me as we drove out to go fishing, to a room full of millionaires—the RYNO journey had been anything but straight and easy. By this point I'd laid off all of the company's employees, including myself. I had to leave my swanky downtown apartment, and was renting a room in my buddy's house. Most of my work consisted of going into the office to support software testing with a few engineers who stayed on for stock options.

The speaking tour was yet another opportunity to stay in the game.

Walking into the hotel, I only had a few thousand dollars to my name. The advance from these gigs would at least help me build up my cash reserves a bit. At the end of the tour, I would receive the second half of the payment, along with a little breathing room.

For months I'd been planning how to ship the RYNO to the hotel. I was using our normal freight forwarder that had seamlessly shipped bikes to Dubai, Hong Kong, and Taiwan. I explained to the agent how important it was for the bike to be there *the day before* my talk—stressing how the bike was the star of the show. I even offered to rent a storage unit in Stockholm the week before to assure it would be there in time. He said no worries, it will arrive at the hotel by midday the day before the talk.

Gillian and I slept in, got up, and went to meet the production manager and his team. This was the first time I'd seen Gillian in this kind of professional environment—how kind and engaging she was with everyone we met. They all loved her.

The moment we walked into the ballroom is when everything hit me—this was a huge deal, way bigger than I originally thought. The room was two stories high, and looked like a set from a Puccini opera. The proscenium around the stage had carved figurines, the ceiling was a gorgeous example of sculpted plaster filigree, and marble columns outlined the room's perimeter.

The crew was rigging three gigantic plasma TV monitors above the stage. There were teleprompter monitors down along the front, video cameras everywhere, and a state-of-the-art sound system. I felt a rush of exhilaration and terror.

The production manager greeted us kindly, then quickly asked when the bike was going to show up.

"Midday," I said, and added that I already let the hotel know so they could tell the delivery team where to set it.

"Midday is now," the production manager countered. He wasn't too happy.

I told him I'd check back as soon as I had an ETA. He relaxed a little, and before he walked off invited us to an early dinner.

I wanted to stay close to the hotel, so Gillian and I went for a short walk along the harbor to find lunch. As we rounded the other side, a huge crowd was forming along the cobblestone street that ran around the harbor. Before we could ask what was going on, a full-on parade started coming around the corner—costumed horsemen with headdresses topped with feathers, the clapping sound of horse hooves on stone, ornate carriages with dignitaries waving, even the royal carriage with the king and queen of Sweden right there at eye level. I asked someone what the occasion was, and she said it was a national independence holiday, similar to our Fourth of July. In the midst of the clamor, my thoughts went to one place—the expected delivery of the RYNO bike.

"Fuck," was all I could muster under my breath. I looked at Gillian. She looked at me with the same *oh fuck* look. We both instinctively turned around, and headed back to the hotel.

By now it was 3 o'clock. I'd checked in with the hotel a half dozen times. No communication with the delivery team, and zero sign of a delivery truck. I checked email on my phone. No updates. I went back to the room, and checked email on my laptop. Then I started sending emails to my shipping coordinator. The clock hit 4 p.m., and I went into full-on regulated panic. I lay on the bed in a frozen stupor. The phone rang. It was the production manager. He wanted to know where the bike was.

Gillian suggested the WiFi might be better in the hotel lobby—we left the room and headed downstairs. Since we weren't using a shipper like FedEx, we couldn't just use a tracking number. I went through all my old emails to the shipper looking for a phone number, or a European contact. There was literally nothing.

It was almost 6 p.m. when the production manager walked up with the crew. "Dinner," he chimed as he slowed his pace a bit, almost walking by. I tried to act as calm as possible as we walked out into the street, and caught up with him.

"Look," he said to me. "I need some odds. What are the chances this bike is going to get here?"

"Fifty-fifty," I said.

"That sounds optimistic," he replied. "Just so you know," he went on, "if the bike doesn't get here, I'm going to cancel your part of the show."

At dinner, Gillian was a rock star. She'd been practicing as a therapist for the last few years, but her inner-LA-video-producer snapped back online. If it wasn't for her, the sound of crab legs cracking open would have been all we heard. She kept the conversation going, and the mood light, even while a dark cloud hung over the table. She was a pro at figuring out groups like this—the power dynamics, authority structure, who we could count on. She used it to her advantage, and strung a nice little web around us all.

Just as we finished ordering, I got my first reply from the shipping company. "Will check to see what's going on," was all it said. My first thought for a reply was, "We need this figured out pretty quickly." But before I hit send, Gillian asked to see what I wrote.

"You mind if I edit this a bit?" she asked.

I handed her my phone.

"I want this elevated to the highest level of management in your company," she wrote. "I need the cell phone number of your VP of global logistics. I need someone to call me immediately. I hope you understand what is at stake here if this shipment isn't delivered today!"

With joking raised eyebrows, I looked at her and hit send.

On the walk back to the hotel, the production manager pulled me aside.

"My phone will be by my bed all night," he said. "In the morning, I think you should drive to the airport, and try to get the bike yourself. Remember, you go on at 10 a.m."

Back in our room, Gillian paced while I talked with the VP of logistics. Apparently, an affiliate shipping company in London was set up to enter the tax number, pay the fee, and release the bike. I got the number, and called them directly—to my surprise someone answered. It was 10 p.m. now. Showtime was 12 hours away.

"How can you be so calm?" Gillian asked when I got off the phone.

I leaned in to kiss her, and peeled off my shirt. She knew exactly where this was going. I grabbed her by the shoulders, and pushed her down on the bed. She unsnapped the top of her jeans. I almost pulled her off the bed as I yanked them down past her ankles. I slid my hand under her ass, and heaved her back up.

"So this is it," she said. "Our first time, under these conditions?"

"Welcome to my world," I said.

The way she grabbed my cock always turned me on. A few firm yanks, and I slowly pressed into her. Our bodies descended into deeper and deeper connection. The sounds she made were a somatic, visceral reminder of how alive she was. We were finding, accepting, and opening to each other like hacking through the brush with a machete.

I started to give her everything I had, and she took it, again and again. Her decisive movements and strength showed me she was with me. She didn't hold an ounce of hesitation. It went on like this for an hour. A euphoric feeling of I'M BACK washed over me—how long it had been since I felt so completely embodied with a woman?

We wound down together, and entered into a moment of quiet reflection. Eventually, Gillian fell asleep. I put my hands behind my head, and started to plan what I was going to do tomorrow.

The day had been so wrapped up in worry and logistics, I never got the chance to rehearse my presentation.

☼

Sunrise came quickly at such a northern latitude. Even with blackout curtains, the yellow glow leaked in around 5 a.m., creating an eerie luminescence in the room. I barely slept, if at all. The feeling of our intense erotic encounter was long gone—all I could see ahead of me were the beady eyes of failure as it held my future in its teeth.

Fuck.

I had all the components I needed— a chance to make a major step forward as a speaker, a fantastic girlfriend, a way to stabilize my finances, even a rented Mercedes SUV sitting in the hotel garage, paid for by the conference. After today, I would have 10 days of freedom to do whatever Gillian and I wanted.

Such a weird, powerless feeling: knowing my bike was locked up in customs only 20 minutes—and one value-added tax number—away from me. Approaching was a two-hour window in which the bike would have to magically teleport itself to the stage before the end of the RYNO teaser video, for the live reveal.

I started to inventory my assets. Was everyone on the production team aligned with the same goals? Did they share my focus? After seeing them in action at the table last night, I came to a solid *yes*. Was anyone working against me? Did the production manager secretly want to see me fail? He came right out and said he'd cancel my part of the show. He didn't do it privately, but instead said it loudly enough so his team could hear. Was he just flexing his muscles to send a message about what kind of man he was? Probably. I wrote it off, and believed he trusted me.

And what about customs? Last night I heard one of the hotel managers say something about having to get guitar amps through customs for a famous musician once. Did anyone at this hotel have an angle I hadn't considered?

Then there was the London-based shipping guy, and whatever magic button he needed to press on his computer. I wasn't sure about it last night, and by now I didn't trust it at all. Plus, it was too far removed from my control.

What could I control? All I knew was I needed to be standing offstage an hour before I went on so I could focus on my lines. Otherwise, I was never going to rock the show. That meant there was no way in hell I was driving to the airport to be at customs when it opened. If the shipper guy came through, great. But as I saw it, the drop dead time was 9 o'clock if anyone from the hotel had a chance to get the bike.

Morning opened with a roar of text messages, phone calls, emails with 10 people copied, and the production manager wanting an update every 15 minutes. The London-based shipper made up a lame excuse why the number he entered didn't work—I'd find out later he was lying to me because he didn't think he'd get the value-added tax money back when I left the country.

When 9 o'clock showed its ugly head, I was forced to calmly execute my fallback mission and tell the production manager I was no longer in charge of getting the bike there. I found everyone in the planning room off to the side of the stage. The production manager and his crew were seated at a big *situation room* table, making final timing plans for the show. I noticed two other people, one an older, somewhat sophisticated woman who looked like Katharine Hepburn from *On Golden Pond*, and a handsome, athletic gentleman who stood next to her with his phone to his ear. They kept exchanging glances as he nodded.

Everyone stopped what they were doing and looked at me. I looked at the production manager.

"Listen, I'm out of options. I want you to know I'm releasing control of trying to get the bike here this morning. I'm getting my suit on, and will be standing off stage planning to go on at 10 a.m. unless you tell me not to."

He turned to the older woman.

"Can you get the bike here?" he barked. She turned to the man on his phone.

"Get thirty-five thousand kroners out of the vault, and grab the van," she yelled theatrically. "We're going to the airport."

Before they left, I told the guy to get a knife so he could cut the banding straps, and to bring a screw gun to unscrew the pallet. I gave him my cell number, and they were gone.

Gillian showed up a few minutes later with two coffees. I gave her the update, and said where I'd be waiting to go on. She took a deep breath.

The show kicked off and launched straight into full swing. The host told his stories, then started my introduction. Walking toward the stage, I looked down one last time at my phone. A text popped up from the guy who left to get the bike.

"I have a visual on the bike, the old lady is sweet talking the customs woman."

I calmly walked up onstage. I had one job now—be professional, engaging, and a bit funny. A tough order with what I'd been through in the last 24 hours. Now that it was just the audience and me, I felt surprisingly relaxed. Only two years ago I had done my first PowerPoint presentation in front of angel investors, totally terrified. I got confused so badly I had to stop in the middle and say, "I'm lost."

Funny how we eventually figure shit out, especially when it's standing in the middle of our path.

Forty-five minutes into my segment, they cued the RYNO teaser video. The house lights went down as the three big-screen monitors rolled. In the middle of the video, with literally three minutes to go before I was supposed to reveal the bike, I saw the gorgeous RYNO being rolled onto the side of stage behind a speaker cabinet. The guy who went to the airport was standing next to it—one big smile, and a humble, two-thumbs-up salute.

I nearly burst into tears right there for the pure human spirit of the whole thing.

Gillian and I stayed an extra day at the hotel so we could tour the city and stop at the Vasa Museum, an engineer's must-see destination. What a story of mythic proportions *that* is. A sailing war ship the queen commissioned in 1626. Two years later—after the royalty added a second gun deck, hundreds of ornate carvings, statues, and royal symbols of power—it rolled over in the harbor on its maiden voyage. Talk about micro-managing a project and not listening to the people who knew what they were doing!

With Gillian's Jungian therapist training, and her fascination with ancient culture and ruins, our trip took on a theme of exploring our own mythic selves. A few weeks earlier, I'd bought a white Celtic dress for her, and made her a wreath of red roses as a crown. In between speaking stops, we toured all the ruins and castles we could find—from the Ales Stenar Swedish Stonehenge on the Baltic coast, to every mythic land we passed. She animated her dress in hundreds of photos and videos, her joyous, poetic body filling it like a goddess moving through the heavens. For two glorious weeks we thundered across the countryside in that Mercedes, creating one magical improvisational day after another, each one bleeding into the next.

Getting it Right

In the blur of summertime lunches on the deck, music festivals, dances, and costume parties, from the first day we met, Gillian and I slowly but fiercely woke each other up. I would look at her sometimes, astonished by it all, and think, "Life just isn't going to be long enough."

In any intimate and romantic relationship, I believe there are cosmic reasons two people find one other—to be each other's teachers and growth partners. Gillian and I were working to help one another bring our unique and whole versions of ourselves online. We needed to lovingly and honestly "slap each other in the face" to wake us from our parallel spells of *feeling good*, in order to begin the painfully hard work of discovering what our greatest gifts might be—for ourselves, and for those around us.

I felt like I landed in a relationship with someone who finally celebrated all of me. She was so good at reflecting my strengths, holding a skillful mirror to my unconscious actions, laughing at my jokes, and texting me five times a day with the most ridiculous emoticons anyone could ever imagine. I loved her with all my heart—wide open, wild, and undefended. This was the relationship I had been preparing for my entire life. Without knowing, I was defining a relationship I wanted, then creating *myself* to meet what the relationship asked of me.

I had always looked for ways to trust women not to hurt me, or to hold them accountable somehow. What I felt with Gillian was a deeper awareness: I knew she could manage her own emotions, and the degree to which she revealed herself to me. Through our relationship I learned to trust myself not to be hurt, and I became more comfortable being affected by whatever form the feelings came in: sadness, anger, tears, joy, whatever.

I learned not to be afraid of big emotions. Feeling pain was just a sign that what I was encountering mattered.

In arguments or moments when we were out of sync, my empathy allowed me to sit next to her, to see her experience through her eyes, and not project the idea that I was somehow a victim; I was free to experience all of her, no matter how she came. I opened myself wider to her than to any woman before—freely and without obligation. She did the same. And in the absence of obligation, there was only the shared desire to be near each other.

Eventually, I consciously chose to open all the way to her.

Once we were back from Sweden, the complexities of real life emerged. Before I met Gillian I'd already been seeing a woman once a week named Cathy. I was open with Gillian about wanting to keep seeing Cathy, and assured her it was casual.

As I was getting ready to see Cathy one day, Gillian asked me very directly what it was that I got out of still seeing her.

"I'm helping her restart her sex drive as part of a long recovery after a car accident," I said.

"I asked you what YOU are getting out of seeing her?" Gillian asked, looking right at me.

That question stopped me cold. I tried to explain how I was good at helping women feel safe, and how it felt good to know I was helping Cathy open back up. But truthfully, I didn't really know what the benefit was for me.

Gillian asked me if she could offer her thoughts.

"From the way I heard you describe your earlier challenges trying to please women," she said, "you might want to get clear on why." Then, in the most respectful way I could have imagined, she added, "You're free to make whatever choice you want, but just make sure it's conscious."

As my primary interest in Gillian progressed, I had to start communicating this awareness to Cathy. She was supportive of whatever was good for me, and offered that she and I were "just rolling along in first gear." Even as Cathy said it, I wasn't convinced it was that clean—for her or for me. As it turned out, it wasn't.

A little time went on. Gillian was supposed to leave town on a two-week business trip, but had to change her flight last minute. When she told me, I explained how we wouldn't see each other until later that night, because I'd be seeing Cathy first. Part of my arrangement with Cathy was that we promised not to change dates once we set them. I was already getting ready to head to her place.

At Cathy's, I tried to explain what was happening. I hoped we could change our plans to just have dinner. Then I'd head off to see Gillian, and Cathy and I could reconnect tomorrow. Cathy wasn't going to have it.

"We need to hold to our agreements," she said. She'd been through some harassment at work recently, and was in the middle of really standing up for herself with good boundaries. I respected what she was saying, but felt stuck hopelessly in the middle.

The evening went by in a blur. I wasn't present for any of it. I could feel myself drifting like a boat in the ocean, waiting for the wind to blow me in some direction. At one point, I fantasized about calling it off and going over to Gillian's. Not a very stoic thing to do.

After saying goodbye to Cathy, I called Gillian to see how she was. It was late. Her voice on the other end was tentative. After a few questions, she admitted her disappointment in me, and the fact that she was more than just a little pissed off—literally coughing up feathers for how unsafe she suddenly felt.

I spiraled into a familiar pattern—all my old shit came right up to the surface. I thought Gillian was trying to manipulate and guilt me into seeing things her way. To confront this urge, I fought to not go back to a pattern of giving up my power. In the process, I became confrontational.

She responded by sharing some very frank and honest insights on how she felt. Sadly, I took a defensive stance. Things spiraled—or at least I did. She heard everything I had to say, but calmly offered that she wasn't sure she was interested in this level of drama in a relationship.

"Do you need emotional confrontations to feel alive?" she asked at one point. Wow! No one had ever been calm enough in a confrontation with me to be so insightful.

Overwhelmed, I asked for a few days to clear my head.

After respecting my time off request, Gillian sent me this heartfelt email:

Dear Chris,

To the one who is quietly and fiercely finding his song, I see you.

In the bloodied-warrior battle-cry for a truth which insists on standing solid and free in its own incarnation—I see you.

In the celebration of your great laughter, and in your fear that it's still not enough and how something in you refuses to live one moment of this life for anyone or anything else other than everything that is your heart – I see you.

Gillian

Receiving her note, and remembering that Gillian was a bit suspicious of chronic and heightened drama, I chose to meet our conflict as a healthy challenge instead of being overwhelmed by my fear of disconnection. I thought, "Okay, so here's a strong and clear-headed woman offering honest reflection. Maybe she's not trying to manipulate or shame me."

To meet that level of feminine potency, I had an important decision to make. I could stay in my old story, or I could finally say "fuck all that shit" to my fears of failure, and of being taken advantage of. I could simply meet Gillian face-to-face with love in real time.

I was coming to grips with the idea that fear could no longer control me. At that moment I could choose to believe in love instead.

Today I recognize the immense significance of this awakening. Amazingly, it took until I was nearly 60 years old to understand how strong a grip my unconscious fear had on me. The fear was centered on feeling overwhelmed when someone would exaggerate the negative effects of my actions, and then shame me for why I was doing it.

Gillian never shamed me for anything. She simply and respectfully drew attention to the effect my actions had on her. I then had the choice to do whatever I wanted with that information. This approach let me choose to cherish her feelings on my own accord if that was what I wanted to do—not because I was being manipulated to do so.

The way I previously dealt with guilt was to fight over how I either didn't do the thing in the first place, or argue that my actions weren't *that bad*. What I've come to discover is that by owning my actions, and then focusing on the impact they actually have on someone I love, I am able to stay awake to the consequences. In turn, this leads me to make better choices in the future.

There are always unique variables why we do things. It's part of who we are. By owning our actions, we're free to focus more curiosity on *why* we do them. It becomes our own inquiry, not someone else's to manipulate.

I say this to help others recognize the deep soul work and courage required to accept the fact that we all have the right to take whatever actions we want in life, as long as we remain accountable for their effects.

When our actions negatively impact someone, we have a powerful choice: to offer the type of empathy that allows us to sit next to them and see the world through their eyes. It takes courage to share the experience of another, and be radically present to how the feeling lives inside them.

Our openness to love is not a promise to carry anyone's feelings for them, or a need to do anything to help them. We simply make a pledge to *ourselves* while respecting their existence. We pledge to honor their experience and, if we choose, to be changed by it.

In this way of loving, fear has no place to hide. We simply choose how to be impacted by others as we evolve and learn from our relationships. We are free to navigate as we hold gratitude towards each person for their gift of honestly sharing in an emotional or intimate encounter, and the joy of being part of yet another experience of human creative expansion.

The day I met Gillian at this level was the day our relationship changed forever. I never went back to my old dynamic. Our commitment to one another's wellbeing became our highest priority—an expression of true, un-enmeshed love.

It wasn't just a shift—it was a complete reprogramming of my approach to confrontation. I went from defending myself, to listening with curiosity. Gillian had modeled for me what a woman who has my best interests in mind really feels like.

My gift to *her* was the chance for her to finally love a man the way she always wanted to love.

"No other man has really known what to do with me," she said. What she loved the most was my ability to call her out of the shadows, and let her know it was safe to show up as her truest self.

Life Contains an Ending

As our relationship approached its one-year anniversary, Gillian and I realized we both had been hiding from the world inside our "bliss cave." I actually put a sheer white curtain up around our bed and called it that. There's nothing wrong with allowing time in one's life to celebrate falling in love and just recharging. But deep down, we both sensed we were heading into new expansive phases of our lives—phases that would require our full attention, and the courage to step into a new way of being.

In Stephen Jenkinson's hauntingly insightful book, *Die Wise*, he writes about how people are afraid to even talk about death, fearing that talking about it signals the beginning of their dying.

My feeling is the opposite: not until we come to grips with our dying, do we change our relationship to living.

If we were given an extra year to live, how would we live differently? It's a strong reminder to be conscious of how we fall asleep in life, how we wish we had another chance, and how we may already have the chance we want right NOW. In essence, live each day like tomorrow is your last.

Waking up to life isn't a euphoria; it's a relationship to the harsh, conscious reality of living. The bedrock that joy sits on is actually the grief, loss, and heartbreak of the very life we must open ourselves to. In essence, grief is the price we pay for love. Joy comes through the same emotional opening as grief: we don't get to choose the feelings we experience. It's our receptivity to the vast spectrum of emotions in life that adds color and vibrancy to all of our experiences.

We must learn to feel as comfortable taking in the grief as we are reveling in the joy. The weight of the feelings is the same; if we hide from one, we hide from them all.

Gillian and I finally sat down to talk on a Sunday afternoon, and confront the fact that we might need to walk farther down the road independent of each other. Over the previous few months, she was getting clear on her new offering, The Kingmaker Sessions, where she planned to provide transformational coaching designed for powerful men who wanted to become more potent in their business and personal lives. She was planning to move back to LA to be near the types of clients she wanted to attract.

As for me, I was still knee deep in RYNO, wanted to stay near my daughter in school, and was already writing this book.

Our conversation started innocently enough: we talked about slowly waking each other up, and wondered where things were going. Then our tone shifted. We made frank, honest declarations of each of our own new needs, and how we deserved the highest of ourselves and each other.

I shared that I was struggling to figure out why I felt so unsure about offering my full commitment to our glorious relationship. She listened carefully, then asked if she could offer her insight.

"Sure," I said. She launched into the most eloquent and deeply resonant train of thought I have ever heard.

"You're still in the middle of your initiation," she said. "You can't commit to me now because you don't yet have your sovereignty of self figured out. I'm heading into my own initiation as well."

She continued.

"You left your marriage six years ago, started a global company, and embarked on a hero's journey to discover who you are. You're still deep in the mythic forest, unsure on where your financial security is coming from. Even your book is an enactment to hack your way out of the thicket, but you're not into the world yet. It hasn't told you what it wants from you."

She paused. Then in the most tender and reverent tone of voice, she went on.

"The way you love me, and the way you have called me forth out of my little leaf-covered corner, is the most gorgeous and exquisite gift I have ever received. I had no idea I could be loved like this, could feel myself like this, could *know* myself in this way. I am forever changed, and forever indebted to who you are as a man."

She went on to explain that during the process of refining The Kingmaker Sessions, she found some relationship clarity: she was done with casual. She wanted to be in a committed partnership with a man in his fully activated sovereignty, ready to give his gifts to the world—someone who knew his capacity to find the mystery of a deep, embodied connection.

"There is no person better prepared than you to be this man, Chris," she said. "You are fully equipped for what the world is calling you to become. I've watched you carefully. I've listened to your dreams and aspirations. You have all the tools you need to find your way into the creation you are building." She stopped and looked into my eyes as I tried to comprehend the magnitude of her transmission.

"Gillian, I am so proud of you for the clarity you have found in yourself," I said. "You feel so strong and clear right now. This is how we love each other. This is how we call each other to be the best we can be."

She took a long breath.

"My experience of you and who are you becoming," she started, "is like witnessing absolute magnificence. I want nothing from you, but for you to be the best man you can possibly be. That is what I'm fighting for. You deserve nothing less. We can't commit to each other right now because we don't know if we are converging, or if the future has other plans for us. What I do know is when you find your sovereignty and yourself, at the moment when it's time for your return, I want to meet you."

☼

Perhaps the hardest thing in the world to recognize, and pull off, is having the discipline to leave someone, and trust fully that if a love is meant to be—if paths are meant to converge—then you and your love will find each other again.

The path ahead for us felt so vibrant and uniquely guided, that I feared any attempt to try and manage a way forward would artificially blind us, and somehow disrupt the beauty of it.

Gillian continued, her eyes welling with tears.

"We are initiating each other," she said. "Our current relationship is acting to anesthetize us from the pain involved in claiming our fullest self-actuation. The more we try and stay in the bliss of this interim state, the longer it's going to take to hack our way out of the forest and claim our self-expressions. We have to get on with the work of putting ourselves out in the world. We perform the greatest acts of love for each other by asking for nothing less than our highest excellence."

Talking about separating in the future, and actually *doing* it, seemed miles apart. The logical question was this: depending on whether we separated now or later, would it have the same traumatic effect? Separating now was gutsy. We decided to soften the blow by adding a grace period: to honor the motive to separate, I would move my stuff out her room, and we'd enter a clean, no-contact radio silence for two weeks. Then we'd reconnect once more before going our separate ways.

That night we made love, crying into each other's eyes, fucking one another awake and alive to what we needed to do, burning everything we could feel deep into the tissue of our long-term memories.

The feeling was like when you have something important to say to someone, and you know they may not like it or take it right. You struggle with different ways to say it, different approaches to put it in the right frame of reference. Then you finally just get frustrated and blurt, "I have something important to say, can I just be totally honest with you?" When they say it's okay, you just speak straight from your heart, clear and true.

That's what happened while we fucked, but it came from deep inside my body.

As that transmission came over me, I whispered to her, "Something is happening to me. Can you feel it?"

"Yes," she said. "I feel it too."

"I need to be totally honest with you."

Then with her acceptance, my body dropped into an exquisite state of unwavering honesty with her. I melted into a bowl. Any drive I had to be anything but in total reverie of the moment dropped away like a robe falling off as you step into the moonlight. I felt totally naked in body and soul, held by the joy of her soft, witnessing gaze.

The profound part was I started fucking her *from* that place—my wildest undefended heart. I could feel my whole body and psyche re-align to this new and powerful expression of honesty. As I continued, my thrusting slowed down to a deliberate and very intentional form of appreciation. I was letting her know in no uncertain terms just how present I was to being open and connected to the very essence of who *she* was. We knew each other so deeply by then, meeting at this place was as close as I'd ever been to another human soul in my entire life.

Without a release I let the energy fade to a quiet peace and tranquility. I lay on her and gave her all my weight. Our breathing slowed. We held each other as we drifted off to sleep.

Handing Each Other Back

A week into our two-week radio silence, Gillian texted me to come by and get my stuff out of her house while she was at work. When I got there the house was pristinely clean, the bliss cave curtain was gone, and all of our costume bins were neatly piled by the front door. The little altar we kept next to her bed, always a bit cluttered with daily life, was now spotless—a crystal heart placed in the middle, and a pair of tiny porcelain deer standing next to each other off to the side.

I sat down, wrote Gillian a note, and left it on the altar, along with a fresh cut orange rose, a symbol of our first date in the Portland Rose Garden:

Dearest Gillian,

You have earned my everlasting devotion.

From here, my love for you comes simply out of the question, "What would love do?"

Thank you for opening your heart to me with such grace, inspiration, crashing courage, and devotion to expand into what our love asked of us.

I kneel before you, and honor you for receiving everything I tore out of my heart, and heaved into your body and soul. For seeing me so fully, then handing my heart back to me wrapped in your profound joy.

The oneness we created together lives in each of us now as two halves. I will cherish my half of that beauty for the rest of my life. Should you ever need to revisit it along your life's journey, I make it available to you as a refuge.

I offer you back now to the wild spirits who brought you to me. I look them softly in the eyes as they take your hand. To them I humble myself as well, and lower my body to the earth in a deep soulful expression of gratitude—for trusting me with your care, and believing in me enough to be worthy of your teachings.

Over the last week I have watched the Temple fire burn down what we have offered it. I now look at the glowing embers. A savage peace lingers there as I turn to walk away. Heart aching and splitting wide open, with a slow motion pivot I face what is in my future.

As a long low exhale of renewal leaves my chest, I lift my chin up to look at a glorious horizon. I pull my shoulders back and walk now toward that light with a newfound love for myself.

I give you all my strength, Gillian, as you walk into your future, into the dreams you have for yourself, into your new wild adventure.

We will always be "SO GOOD!"

Love you,

Chris

Two Candles

After two weeks of not talking, the day of reconnection was upon us. We chose the Rose Garden—home of our first date.

I suggested a ritual: we'd each buy a candle, and decorate it to symbolize what our relationship meant. The plan was to set the candles next to each other, light them, then reflect on our relationship while we watched the other person's candle burn. To finish, we'd blow the other person's candle out.

That whole day I was terrified. When I texted Gillian to finalize the plan, she said she was afraid too.

At 5 o'clock, I parked and walked up to her car. She stepped out as I approached. Just seeing her made my heart almost pound out of my ribcage.

We drifted tentatively forward until we stood across from each other. I leaned in, and pulled her to my chest. My breathing took on a wild, heavy, moaning sound, each exhale ripping out of my throat. We lingered, frozen there waiting for the feeling of missing each other so terribly to subside.

We walked to the spot where we spent our first afternoon together. The ground was soft and a bit muddy from the spring rains. I stood there for a second trying to stay in my body.

"This is so weird," I said. "How is the temperature so neutral? No wind? Or is it that I can't even feel myself right now?"

Gillian said she felt exactly the same, like she was walking in a different dimension.

We set out a blanket and shared a few snacks, which helped us find ourselves. We thanked each other for our kindness, and reflected on how beautiful our relationship had been. But when she said "our souls met each other," I lost it. I pitched over and grabbed a rolled-up blanket to cover my mouth. She held me as I wailed. It was the hardest I'd cried since I heard about Dave Lee's suicide.

Gillian never wavered in the fact that we were mid-stream in our separation. She never took my displays of grief to mean anything other than a sign of how much we loved each other, and the pain of moving through this.

After an hour we decided it was time to light our candles. We packed up the picnic stuff first—we wanted the candles to be our last act.

She took her candle out first, handed it to me, and quietly explained what she'd been through these last couple of weeks. The candle was wrapped in fabric torn from the white scarf she wore at Burning Man. My mind flashed to it wrapped around her naked body, blowing in the dusty wind. Tied to the fabric was a chrome tag. The inscription read, "Because we become more beautiful when we are broken."

The candle itself was something she'd created from raw beeswax—a perfect cylinder she cut into two halves and pressed back together. It was a symbol of our separation. She painted the crack between the halves with gold eyeliner. I held it in the palm of my hand for a while in stunned silence.

My candle, a tall glass jar style, represented the many costumes we made together. I wrapped it in scraps of white fur, pulled a piece of black fishnet stocking over it, and plucked the fur through the holes in the stocking to form tufts. In the middle I set a jeweled silver heart under the stockings—as if the heart was being held in a cage. I hot-glued gold fringe around the bottom, added a row of chrome studs, and topped the candle off with a gold braided rope around the opening.

We set them side by side. I stood up nervously. I knew what I wanted to say, but struggled with my right to say it. Finally, I found the words:

"Gillian, at such a potent junction of my personal history, a memory that will last I'm sure for the rest of my days, I have to ask you because I couldn't help *but* ask…what do you think about going back to your house and making love one more time?"

Gillian looked long and hard at me.

"I can't," she said. "I don't want to reset the whole last two weeks of grieving all over again."

"That's okay" I said. "But I had to ask."

"The cards!" she exclaimed, remembering the Tarot deck in her bag. She pulled the deck out, shuffled it, and set it for me to cut. Together we spread the cards across the one little blanket we hadn't packed yet, and each pulled a card to represent what was coming next in our lives.

I slid my hand along the cards from the left until I settled on one near the middle. When I turned it over, it was the "World" card – a naked woman dancing in an open portal, the last card in the Major Arcana, a sign of both completion and renewal, a pause before the next big thing.

Gillian's eyes grew wide.

"You're on your way, my love," she smiled.

She ran her hand over the cards, reached and pulled the "Hermit." He stands alone on the top of a mountain with a lantern in his hand. He has attained his spiritual pinnacle, and is ready to share his knowledge with others.

Gillian held the card for a moment, then set it down.

"We are both being initiated into something powerful," she said. "But neither of us can possibly know what it is from where we sit now."

It was getting dark outside. We looked at the candles and asked if it was time to light them. Stories ran through my mind about respecting Gillian's wishes, being stoic, staying dependable—easy distractions to keep me away from the deep urgency I felt to take Gillian back to her house.

I didn't want it to end like this.

I was still feeling the echoes of grief. I asked myself, "What is my motivation for asking her again? What do I hope to achieve?" The answer I kept getting pointed back to was a sense of responsibility to lead us out of this sorrowful impasse, and back to the roads we both needed to find. I wasn't trying to rescue us from this—I was trying to build out of it.

I looked at her.

"I need to ask you one more time about going back to your house. I believe I can create an encounter that will lead us out of this sadness and into our individual futures."

She sat quietly for a moment to reconsider her position.

"I have always trusted your leadership" she said. "If you feel like this is the right thing to do, that's what we'll do."

"Thank you," I said.

Calling Forth Our Futures

Driving back to Gillian's house, I felt a deep sense of responsibility and call to lead. I knew what we'd been building together was no longer sustainable, or in alignment with where we wanted to go. It reminded me of the lead-up to leaving my marriage: not the angst and frustration, but the devotion to making sure my family and I made it to a place of safety.

How was I going to position the ending of *this* in a way that would give us the best chance at our new futures?

In her bedroom, we placed our unlit candles on the bedside altar. Then I stripped out of my clothes, folded them neatly, and placed them on the floor against the wall. When she walked in from the bathroom, I asked for her permission to get into her bed.

"Of course," she said.

We disappeared into a haze of erotic connection that celebrated who we were, reminded us of our love, and reconnected us to the familiar feelings of our relationship container. We tore our hearts out, then handed them to each other—over and over.

At one point, she energetically took my cock and started fucking me *back* with it. I felt it coming on and surrendered to HER leadership, allowing myself to feel the love she had for me. She fucked me deeply and exquisitely with my own cock—full of passion, love, and a devotion that she knew may never come again.

I felt absolutely loved in that moment by this woman who'd had my back from the first day. Not only had it, but climbed up on it, and even bit my shoulders when she had to. A woman who remembered everything I'd ever said to her, who reflected my love for her back to me, and showed me things about myself I didn't know were there.

When we finally wound down, we fell into a long, timeless embrace. Everything began to shift into a liminal fog. We drifted weightlessly in her bed, floating between worlds. Every clock in that house stopped ticking in our honor.

As I came back to the living, I felt my second purpose rekindle in me. I still had a potent responsibility to complete. I leaned over to her.

"Do you feel that? The earth is loosening around our entwined roots?"

"Yes."

"I'm going to fuck you now like we are slowly peeling each other apart," I said.

We sat up and pushed at each other to feel our weight. She had my hard cock in her hand. We tumbled from one end of the bed to the other. She finally draped her body half-off the bed, one hand on the floor.

We were no longer making love as an investment in our relationship, no longer pouring concrete around the foundation of who we were together. Now we were walking forward into the mystery, holding our cards, and moving as individuals.

Something odd began to happen. There was a sense that by loving each other as individuals, and not as a couple, it actually felt stronger than being in a relationship. I have always been a relationship-centric person; this feeling made me wonder why I'd carried so much attachment to that kind of union for so long. Maybe it's healthy for couples to burn down an old relationship dynamic from time to time so they can recreate something new.

Gillian was completely and utterly synchronized with everything I felt. We were creating this together. She made sure I knew where she stood by how she fucked me back. We were loving each other open to new lives—*awake* to who we were as fully expressed human beings, and *away* from a relationship that no longer served us. We took what the other offered and recreated it, held it like a hot iron over an anvil. We forged it, one loving blow after blow, into something new.

As our exchange swept into oblivion, I pulled her back up on the bed.

"I am totally transformed," I said. "My grief is gone. I feel so awake and alive. Can you feel it too?"

She just let out a long, low, whistling breath.

"I'm at peace," I said. "Are you ready to light the candles?"

She lowered her gaze and moved to sit on the floor. We lit our candles, placed them in front of us, and watched them burn down, lingering in their flickering flames. There was such a peace hanging in the air, like the curtain had come down on a breathtaking show, the kind where the audience sits in stunned silence before breaking into applause.

The candles out, we rolled into bed and pulled the sheets up to our chins.

I lay awake for a while. Tomorrow I'd walk out another door—into yet *another* unknown future. I'd been on this road before... but a different man inhabited my body now.

I marveled at how far Gillian and I had come together, and how we'd called each other out of our shadows.

I thought about my daughter. She was doing so well for herself, had fought all the bureaucracy of filling out applications for student loans and housing, had a great apartment, was in school to be a video game developer.

I thought about my ex-wife. She'd gone back to school, and loved her new job. The last time we spoke, she said she was happy. She even thanked me for the courage it took to walk out, admitting we were totally broken.

RYNO had just had a breakthrough, finally acquiring the patent rights we needed from a stubborn inventor, allowing us to offer a licensing deal to a large Asian manufacturer.

I wondered, had I done everything I could to help Gillian be as ready as possible for the bright future that was coming? Had I done everything I could for myself and my own future? Was I at peace enough to let go of our love, and to trust its own autonomous freedom?

Gillian woke before me. She brought me coffee in bed—part of our morning ritual. I had a hard time taking in the gesture without losing it.

When it was time, she walked me to the front door. The same swelling feeling that came over me at the park was back. Our hearts beat in unison, just six inches away.

"I don't know when we'll see each other again," I said. "When we do, I don't know if it will ever feel the same."

She nodded in silence.

I stepped back to look at her one more time. Life's meaning isn't about what we try to create and force on the world—it's about how we allow ourselves to be changed by the act of creation.

We do everything we can to be available to the creative collaboration between "who we are" and "who we need to become," all in an effort to give our creative work its best shot at becoming what it needs to be. It's like winding up the creative spring in a big spinning top as tight as we can, until the day comes where, like with our grown children, our best works of art, or a big, fat love, we press the release button. We give it a little shove, and watch it spin on its own like a fierce, swaggering bull into the china shop of the world.

In that exalted moment, we stand holding our breath, lingering as the weightless ambiguity takes hold, something between the thundering majesty of our creation, and the choking grief of it being over. All the while, we know we are one step closer to our freedom, and our ultimate liberation.

I walked through that front door.

Descending down the front steps, I turned once more to smile up at Gillian. She smiled back through her tears as she arched her hand in a wide sweeping wave goodbye.

ACKNOWLEDGEMENT

Having barely made it out of high school, with no ability to even spell or know what a complete sentence was, I knew I had to find a male editor that could somehow pull this all together and be a hard-ass coach to wrestle any sign of "the Chris show" into submission. I finally found Dave Jarecki through my amazingly talented book cover designer and author resource, Lieve Maas.

Dave was the perfect find, with his own baseball hero's journey and the hard-won reclamation of his passion as a writer. I asked him at the beginning what he thought of my work. He answered, "I don't know yet. It's like looking at a bunch of jigsaw puzzle pieces. I'm trying to find the corners." He bravely put on his editor headlamp and spelunked through my first few sketchy iterations. He always emerged from these early descents with kindness, encouragement, requests for more context, and terrific improvements to the emerging book. As the book began to take form, he did a masterful job at finding a sub-plot and rearranging the stories into sections with a common thread of meaning or symbolism.

As the book became more focused, my girlfriend at the time, Gillian, who is a Jungian oriented psychotherapist, stepped in as executive bullshit filterer. Gillian is formerly an LA advertising and media producer, but in her true nature, she's a quiet-yet-wild creature from the hinterlands, one foot in the underworld, one in the real world.

In her practice, she offers a series of experiential sessions for men called The Kingmaker Sessions. With this expertise at hand, I was exposed to a treasure trove of insight into my own self-awareness, psyche, and unconscious shadows. I can assure you, the experience of diving headfirst into a life-long collection of erotic stories reflective of various levels of dating skill, sitting inches away on the couch from my Jungian-psychotherapist girlfriend, sure stirred a few heated moments. I spent many long hours squirming in the "hot seat" as she unflinchingly kept the light on me until I was willing to look my ego, shadow, or questionable motivations squarely in the eye. Gillian's fiery passion, and deep compassion and respect for the masculine psyche, have made this a better book—and me a better man.

Lastly, thank you to all the women and men in each of these stories. Your participation in these encounters and experiences allowed me to see myself in new and more complete ways. I am forever grateful to each one of you.

Senior Editor:
Dave Jarecki
dave@davejarecki.com

Book Cover Design:
Lieve Maas
lieve@brightlightgraphics.com

Meaning Excavator:
Gillian Pothier
gillianpothier@gmail.com

Author:
Chris Hoffmann
chris@hoffmann.world

www.ingramcontent.com/pod-product-compliance
Lightning Source LLC
Chambersburg PA
CBHW020252170426
43202CB00008B/335